AYURVEDA

AYURVEDA

The Food Balancing Act

BRYAN OSBORNE

JANUS PUBLISHING COMPANY
London, England

First published in Great Britain 2000
by Janus Publishing Company Limited,
76 Great Titchfield Street,
London W1P 7AF

www.januspublishing.co.uk

**A CIP catalogue record for this book
is available from the British Library.**

ISBN 1 85756 408 1

Phototypeset in 11.5 on 13.5 Baskerville
by Keyboard Services, Luton, Beds

Cover design John Anastasio

Printed and bound in Great Britain

by the same author:
Say I Am with Raja Yoga
Victory to Vinoba   Vinoba Bhave: A Social Reformer

Contents

Introduction

Ayurveda is the ancient Indian system of medicine and diet. Medicine and diet are so closely linked as to be inseparable. The word 'Ayurveda' is made up of two parts, both of which are symbolic. *Ayur* means 'life', and *veda* means 'knowledge', giving us 'the knowledge of life', and portraying a particular attitude to all living things.

Ayurveda is believed to be the oldest medical system in the world, reaching back to around 5,000 BC. It was in existence in the north of India, where people from the west, from Europe, had moved across the vast stretches of land on conquering missions, subsequently meeting with the people who were already there. This process happened over a long period, and resulted in the mixing of Aryan and Indian cultures, producing what is now considered as the Indus Valley civilisation of India, with its highly developed city states.

Ayurveda is used today by 80 per cent of the population of India, which is close on 800 million people, but not all of those are able to take advantage of it fully.

This book aims to extend the knowledge that is available in the various textbooks on Ayurveda and, at the same time, to expose and explain some of the body's mysteries that are found in both ancient and modern books on the subject.

According to Ayurveda, incorrect or insufficient diet is the cause of virtually all conditions of being unwell and of disease. Everyone needs food but Ayurveda says that diet is the main factor in this world of cause and effect. Therefore, all is diet, and there is nothing else. Ayurveda focuses on the healing power of herbs and plants, in a system of medicine, health and food. But first comes food and diet.

More and more people today are beginning to realise that a different approach to health and medicine needs to be taken, although much progress has been made over the past decade or so.

At its very heart, Ayurveda can be described as spiritual in its absolute conviction of linking the wholeness of the universe, to the oneness within the human body. This connection between nature, as we know it and the universe is the basis for all Ayurveda principles of healing and medical knowledge.

In India, Ayurveda methods of treating medical conditions, with their emphasis on the complete linkage of our diet with the workings and the healthy state of the body reaches back thousands of years. The ancient literature of India, the *Vedas* and the *Upanishads*, stress the importance of purity in food. From those writings we acknowledge the numerous saints, seers, or *rishis*, who have provided us with the necessary knowledge and wisdom, giving us the foundations to work on. Most of this ancient wisdom and philosophy was passed on verbally and only at a later stage was this fund of wisdom and knowledge, including Ayurveda, recorded in Sanskrit, the classical language of India.

In the *Upanishads* we are told that purity of food leads to purity of the spirit and of our very being. We are indeed what we eat; the *rishis* of ancient India were themselves human beings, and understood that it was good for everyone to obtain a high standard of right and pure food. This was not meant for the few, but a goal to be reached by all.

Ayurveda can be described as making use of nature, giving back and restoring to people what is natural and what belongs to them in the first place, as a birthright. It provides a balance in diet and food, taking into account the type of constitution of each person.

Indian philosophical systems and teachings emphasise the importance and recognition of the Supreme Being. At the same time they state that the universe is the macrocosm and mankind the microcosm of this Supreme Spirit or Absolute and that there is a direct relationship between the two at all times. This relationship can be realised, by the practical application of methods running throughout the Indian approach to philosophy and thought.

Today we can still enter into a spiritual realisation and a philosophy which will offer us a path to understanding the urgent matters of health and well-being, in the context of our present situation.

At the 55th Plenary Session of the All-India Ayurveda Congress held in New Delhi in July 1998, the Indian Prime Minister Mr A B Vajpayee, praised Ayurveda and said that the system was capable of curing disease by attacking the root cause. During the 10th International Congress on Immunology held at New Delhi in November, 1998, the President of India, Mr K R Narayanan, called upon scientists to develop alternative systems of medicine. He said that these alternatives, including Ayurveda, were holistic, curative and preventive, and dealt with the subtle relationship between body, mind, and the environment. The President continued, 'It has been said that the Indian system of medicine, Ayurveda, if rejuvenated, and subjected to severe scientific analysis and tests, could perhaps give a holistic dimension to modern medicine.'

Ayurveda deals with things as they are; the science is the result of many thousands of observations noted over a long time. Clearly, vegetables and fruit are good and healthy foods to eat, but there must be some balancing and discrimination in all food. Often what will suit one person may affect others differently. In Ayurveda, there is a balancing act. You will discover your type of constitution later in this book and will therefore know your dominant forces, and you can act accordingly. One of the unique personalities of the twentieth century, Vinoba Bhave, the renowned Indian social reformer, once remarked that he did not deal in opinions but only in thought, where there can be give and take. In Ayurveda, we are considering things for what they are, and not as a matter of opinion, or according to the fad or the current flavour of the month.

My friend Joan is not well. She suffers from aches and pains in the joints, and on top of that does not sleep very well. Yes, Joan has seen her doctor, but other than receiving a few pills to help her get a good night's sleep, nothing much has changed in her arthritic condition. The aching joints are still there, and have not improved during the past few months. Questions are beginning to be asked about the how, the when, and the why of disease. For example, why has Joan aching joints to begin with? There is in our National Health Service good treatment available for conditions and illnesses, but little help in finding ways of preventing forms of disease and discomfort arising in the first place.

Ayurveda, the codified system of health in India, gives us vital clues leading to explanations for the need to balance food and diet in our daily living. It is a lifestyle to maintain good health and what, in Indian terms, can be translated as reaching a state of wellness, or well-being.

The facts are there for all to see, recorded in the ancient books on Ayurveda, and continuing up to the present day. The path of Ayurveda can help uncover the secrets of the body, and what makes it work. It aims to give a fuller dimension in dealing with the question of being healthy, and the reasons for being unhealthy. We know the feeling of being off colour, unfit, not up to the mark. Various conditions or symptoms can exist from time to time, sometimes continually. Often this state cannot at the beginning be recognised as being a specific disease at all.

Ayurveda puts forward a range of factors leading to a healthy life allowing us to become more in tune with nature and the environment. Diet and good digestion are the main building blocks that we can use. On this sure foundation, the theory and practical application of Ayurveda is based.

Although the nutritional value in food is vitally important, proteins, carbohydrates fats, salts and the like, Ayurveda recognises that there are many qualities in food. These include the vitamin content, which is invaluable and indispensable. This is needed to repair the constant wear and tear of the body by the assimilation of the extraneous material and nutrients from the food. In Ayurveda, of equal value is maintaining the balance of the three forces that are found in all of nature, the *doshas vata*, *pitta* and *kapha*. There is constant recognition of the other values or inherent qualities in food, whether they are hot or cold, raw or cooked, and also in what combination they are taken. There are foods easily or quickly digested, foods that are harder to cope with, foods that increase the digestive power, and those that bind other foods in the intestines.

These attributes are given to specific foods, including those having the ability to stimulate and to strengthen.

The basic philosophy in Ayurveda is the five-elements theory; all matter, including tissues, organs, diet and the *doshas*, are built upon these. From these elements there evolves the idea of the controlling forces in everything, that is, the three *doshas* of *vata*, *pitta* and *kapha*. These *doshas* act on the body tissues (the *dhatus*), giving rise to various metabolic end-products, the *mala*. The behaviour of all these are controlled by our diet, when we eat our food, how we live our lives, and in what conditions, and last but not least, by our mental states. Anything out of kilter can make us feel unwell, but not necessarily to be suffering from any specific illness. When we remain unwell for too long, however, we are more likely to be open to attack by outside germs or viruses.

Ayurveda shows that the well-being and good health of each person is dependent on the balance of three forces controlling our physical and mental states and activity. These forces are a reflection of the principles of all creation in the universe. The underlying principles not only embrace creation, but also are concerned with preservation and destruction.

There is a certain pattern, a rhythm, in everything in the natural world. Not only do the famous three, the *doshas*, change in their importance and in their dominant positions throughout the life of each person, but also their presence is recognised and controlled by us every year, every month, every season, every day and, in fact, every moment of our lives. We are changing all the time.

Any information or advice given in this book is not to be taken or intended to be a replacement for medical advice. Any person with a condition that requires medical attention should consult a qualified medical practitioner or suitable therapist.

Acknowledgements

Popular Prakashan
Bombay

Vinoba Bhave: Indian Social Reformer
1895 - 1982

1
The Doshas

In Ayurveda, the science of life, the three *doshas*, *vata*, *pitta*, and *kapha*, play a vital role in the maintenance of our health and well-being. All three *doshas*, or forces, are equally important, and have to be kept in balance, so that none of them is allowed to obtain a strength or dominance over the others nor, as in some cases, are two of the *doshas* allowed to obtain a dominance in influence. The problem in trying to put forward a completely intelligent explanation of the *tridosha* theory system is that there is, whether we like it or not, a blending of the two aspects of organic life. You have, on the one hand, the physical and metaphysical and, on the other, the physiological and also the psychological aspects. The more you are able to look into this, the more the line of demarcation may be traced and spotted and differences explained. The Ayurveda practitioner knows and believes that all physiological functions are controlled by the three principles.

Vata
The first of the *doshas* is *vata*, which is given the role of movement and energy and can be equated with that of kinetic energy. The original meaning of the word *vata* is

'that which moves', which fairly sums up its function. *Vata* is the master and maker of all forms of activity, including the communication network of the body, tissue to tissue, cell to cell, also perception, including pain, assimilation and the body's reactions. It is responsible for the messages from the memory to consciousness and transfers current experiences into memories. It is vitally concerned with speech. At the physical level of operations in the body, it is responsible for all major and minor movements say, for walking, for movement of the ovum from the ovary to the Fallopian tube. *Vata* is the vital force and is basically in charge of the other *doshas*, *pitta* and *kapha*.

Charaka, the commentator on Ayurveda at around AD 100, gave a breakdown of *vata* into five categories covering the above descriptions, and these are set down as those movements relating to the chest and respiration; cardiac functions of the chest; the upper gut; the intestines and the churning movements necessary for the digestion of food and in the later formation of the stool. The last category comprises the functions relating to the rectum and genito-urinary system, and evacuation of stools, ejaculation of sperm, and going on to parturition, that is, the delivery of a child.

The main characteristic of *vata* is that of being made up of air and space of the five elements: air, space, earth, fire and water. It is naturally light, cold and dry. *Vata* is much affected by changes in diet, and also with any changes in the weather. *Vata* really has a lot of control over the other *doshas* of *pitta* and *kapha*. It is said that *vata* does not really increase or decrease, but does and can become unbalanced and so lose control over the other *doshas*, thus causing problems. Therefore most of the help and therapy Ayurveda gives to *vata* is concerned with restoring the *dosha* rather than increasing or decreasing its quantity.

From a medical and practical point of view, where there is an imbalance of *vata*, the skin and scalp can become dry, with possibly dandruff in the hair. A lot will depend upon the constitution and age, and a number of other factors can present themselves. These include a lessening of intelligent understanding, loss of some memory, loss of sleep, indigestion, back ache, joint and thigh pains, and feeling the effects of cold and wintry weather. The tendency is for loss of control in *vata* to occur in the case of older people. *Vata* can also be upset during the hot summer months. Stress will unbalance *vata*, as will lack of sleep, over-tiredness and excess of physical activity. *Vata* is seen to be very important and can be described as the chief in charge, and an invisible controlling force within ourselves. In Ayurveda, the other *doshas pitta* and *kapha*, are described and understood at a more physical level. *Vata* is not visible, but certainly exists because of the effects it produces.

Pitta
The next *dosha* is *pitta*, which is responsible for all types of transformation in the body, giving energy and controlling digestion and metabolic functions. The five types of *pitta* are as follows. Firstly *aharapachak*, this controls digestion of food. The second is *ranjak pitta* and controls the colour of the skin and complexion. It needs to be vital and healthy to encourage formation of further tissues. *Sadhak pitta* is the third type of *pitta*, located in the brain and is in charge and responsible for processing impulses that are continually reaching it from the outside environment. Fourthly there is *bhajak pitta* controlling some of the chemical activities of the skin. Lastly there is *alochak pitta*. This remarkable type resides in the eye and is responsible for vision. *Pitta* is responsible for the conversion of light rays which fall on

the retina of the eye, transposing or converting this light into electrical impulses carried by the optic nerve for processing by the brain. We certainly know today that there are some extremely complex processes going on, chemical processes which occur in the rods and core cones of the retina and leading to our sight. In the brain, the *dosha pitta* is responsible for sorting out and analysing data received. Therefore it is concerned with intelligence and includes the qualities of decisiveness, and good maturity in overall comprehension. In this respect, *pitta* will also control such emotions as anger and fear. The character of *pitta* is a positive one, in the main concerned with action. As it controls digestion, it is therefore intimately responsible for appetite, hunger and thirst. It has a direct connection with the look and condition of the hair and skin. This factor will be explained further when we consider later the direct relationship between diet and the *doshas*, leading to our aim of controlling and balancing them.

When compared with *vata*, *pitta* is of a much more physical nature, being the controller of the digestion of our food. In this function, *pitta* works with *vata* to keep the gut moving correctly and normally. Physical movement (energy), controlled by *vata*, and the actual chemical transformation, produced by *pitta* are needed in the action. *Pitta* will also be controlling skin condition and complexion and encouraging formation of further tissues. Another important function of *pitta* is the work it does in the brain, processing the many impulses reaching it from the outside, in other words, environmental factors. The skin is very important in the health of a person and this is another job carried out by *pitta dosha* in its work of controlling the chemical activities of the skin.

Another type of *pitta* is that which is resident in the eye and responsible for our vision. Normally there is no chemical transformation in the senses, such as touch, pain, and taste, although neurotransmitters may be formed. In the case of the *pitta* relating to the eye, a chemical transformation occurs in the eye in a way that a visual impression is made on the retina of the eye. External influences, such as diet and the weather, can disturb *pitta*, which is made up of the elements fire and water. Dominance of *pitta* can give a good glow to the skin, with soft hair, possibly greying, and baldness. It can also result in excessive sweat.

Increase in the *dosha pitta* is usually due to a dietary imbalance, but it can be due to seasonal variations in the weather. Therefore *pitta* is responsible for many conditions relating to our well-being but is also under the continual watchful eye of the boss *vata*.

Kapha
The last of the *doshas* is *kapha*, the kind and gentle one. *Kapha* is sometimes briefly described as phlegm. It is very important as it distributes energy in the body, as well as smoothing out and solving the problems as and when they arrive. *Kapha* is also involved in the construction of the body, from the smallest cell to the largest bone structure. It has the job of holding everything together, a most important function, and is responsible for giving mental strength, and organising defences against disease.

As in the case of *doshas vata* and *pitta*, there are five classifications or types of *kapha*. Firstly, very importantly and enjoyably, *kapha* makes the taste of food possible by way of the saliva, which is called *bodhak*. Next comes the activity that supplies and controls the gut; this is *kledak*. *Shleshak* is the synovial fluid lubricating our joints, and giving suppleness and firmness to ligaments. *Tarpak* lies in the brain and protects it from external injury. The last type is *avalambhak*, the home of which is situated in the thorax and pelvis. This has the job of lubricating organs in those regions, and seeing that they are working correctly.

Kapha, of water and earth elements, has a heavy nature in itself and is therefore both stable and moist. Where there is a surplus of the *dosha kapha*, it will generally give a person gentleness and sweetness, and a tendency towards plumpness, contentment and perhaps a little slowness. But a predominance of *kapha* will also give a strong capability to withstand shocks of a mental and physical nature in the most trying of conditions. Where the *dosha* is deranged there can, of course, be trouble, as will happen if any *doshas* are behaving abnormally, or are out of balance. When this happens with *kapha*, problems arising include emaciation, poor digestion, general weakness and lethargy, and in the longer term, respiratory diseases.

In addition to the overall factors relating to hereditary and the immediate environment, the *doshas* of the individual will vary from day to day. These variations will be caused by a person's activity, diet and psychological conditions. It is generally the case that variations in the three *doshas* are usually quite small, but nevertheless they will have their effect on the human system. How often have we heard the question, 'How are you today?'

A disturbance, or imbalance, of the *doshas* will affect the human system in some way. Often these imbalances will be of a mild nature but, on the other hand, a knowledge of the effects will be valuable for remedial action to be taken. The action needed may require some alteration in the diet, or even some medical action. If you think you have a medical condition, as opposed to following an incorrect diet, or have been unwise in following a certain diet and eating the wrong type of food, you should always consult a registered medical practitioner, telling him or her what dietary procedures you have been following and any other factors that you may feel has had an effect upon your health.

Disturbed *vata* is indicated by excessive thirst, tremors, dryness, redness of skin, hiccough, asthma, problems with the nose and throat, and circulatory troubles, among others. Where the *dosha vata* is increasing, this will give roughness of voice, desire for heat, insomnia, weakness and constipation. In a lessening of *vata*, this will give uneasiness, tiredness, possibly fainting and resulting unconsciousness.

In Ayurveda, the principal aim is to keep the *doshas* happy, so that in general terms the main remedy for too much *vata* is in the application of heat and oil, both externally and internally, so that *vata*'s dryness and cold nature and qualities are counteracted. In both medicine and in food, a salty taste is most important, and will be good for the appetite and digestion, as well as being slightly laxative. Next in line comes the sour and then sweet taste. People with excess *vata* at any particular time should try to relax, have plenty of entertainment and give themselves space, both physically and mentally.

Pitta is hot and an over-abundance of this will need to be cooled. Here, bitter is the important taste followed by sweet and astringent. In these days of aromatherapy, sweet-smelling scents are good and cooling, as well as cool showers and baths. The aim always is to reduce *pitta*'s intensity, so that quiet and meditations will also help in keeping the mind calm, leading to coolness in the body system. As far as diet is concerned, some raw food including salad, can also help.

Disturbed *pitta* can result in burning sensations, excessive heat, perspiration, thirst, irritability, indigestion, sensations of heat in the chest and stomach, stupor and defective vision.

Where *pitta* is increasing, this will again produce burning sensations, a preference for cold foods, insomnia, fainting, and a diminished functioning of the sense organs. Where *pitta* is decreasing, it will produce dull complexion and diminished body heat.

When *kapha* is out of control, there is a tendency towards a natural inertia and lethargy. It therefore needs the pungent taste of fire and air, to control this abundance, followed by the bitter and astringent tastes. Where there is a problem with *ama* (improperly digested food particles being present), then that condition will need to be dealt with in the first place, clearing the channels, so that bitter should be used. This can then be followed by pungent tastes that will strengthen and re-awaken the essential digestive fire, the *agni*. Exercise, fasting, dry and warm clothing will all help decrease *kapha*, and so will hot baths.

Where the *dosha kapha* is disturbed, this will produce heaviness, drowsiness, pallor, nausea, anorexia, loss of memory and rigidity in the joints. An increase in *kapha* will produce a heaviness in the limbs, cold sensations, tiredness, excessive sleep and a pallid complexion. In the case of decreasing *kapha*, dryness, internal burning sensations, empty feelings in the stomach, looseness of the joints, thirst, a sense of weakness and insomnia can be produced.

These conditions and their symptoms are in no way a complete and all-embracing list of the problems associated with the imbalances of the three *doshas*, where there exists an imbalance in just one of the *doshas*. It will also be seen there can be an overlap in the symptoms relating to the *doshas'* imbalance, for example, burning sensations can be produced by increased *pitta dosha*; these can also be present in the case of decreasing *kapha dosha*.

In Ayurveda, great importance is given to diet and the

food we eat each day. Food should be good and pure, eaten in a calm manner, and if possible at the right time of day. As would be expected from Ayurveda, the medicines and drugs used are themselves entirely obtained from naturally produced plants, herbs and medicinal plants, grown not only in India but throughout the world. Food has the same value and effect as the medicinal plants used in Ayurveda medical practice. Plants and herbs have been used success-fully for many thousands of years, so that food is an extension of the grand system in nature, giving the right requirement for keeping the *doshas* in balance.

An interesting aspect of Ayurveda is that, in the strictest sense, it does not instruct or advise on following a fixed or strict diet as far as overall nutrition is concerned, although in the case of imbalance of *doshas* resulting in illness, Ayurveda will recommend a strict diet for a limited period only, or until such time as health has been restored.

What Ayurveda is able to supply is a path forward for people to follow, so that one is able to obtain and retain this balance of the *doshas*. Ayurveda will be able to guide in finding out the right diet at a particular time, taking into account other factors such as type of constitution.

Ayurveda looks upon food as a natural medicine, and the practitioner will only at a later stage give drugs or medicinal herbs if diet alone has failed to give a return to health and freedom from disease. Proper and efficient digestion is equally stressed in Ayurveda. Good and healthy food can also cause problems to our health, if this food is not properly digested, or if it is not correct for the particular time and circumstances. Inefficient digestion will in itself cause a build up of waste products, toxins and improperly digested food, or *ama*, the enemy.

Ayurveda takes into account a number of individual

factors, when giving suggestions or recommendations on diet, including overall constitutional type, personality, the state of current health and well-being, and physical and emotional needs. Your needs will be guided to a certain extent by the work we do and our lifestyle; whether a strong and strictly physical nature is required, or whether physical demands are not great, but rather that they are of a mental nature. Often there will be a mixture of both physical and mental needs in varying proportions.

Human consciousness and mind helps in using our senses in relation to eating habits and diet, and getting the feel for ourselves and our bodies as to the food and diet we are happy with. We can begin to use our own sensory perceptions, much more than we have been used to in the past.

Often we are given contradictory information about food and nutrition, including opinions about our requirements for calories, carbohydrates, fats, protein and vitamins. Ayurveda is aware of all these factors, but at the same time is not over concerned with them.

It is important to know the effect each type and class of food will have on the three *doshas*, the controlling elements in our bodies. It is this subjective response, our act in choosing, the bringing something under our control and power, that is the purpose and power of Ayurveda.

For many people the act of eating is an intuitive operation. This is right and in line with Ayurveda thinking. We like certain foods and we eat them. Our body tells us what we like, particularly through our sense of taste. In other words, for the most part, eating is a practical operation, but for very young children, helped and guided by their parents.

We are in the end guided in food preferences by a number of factors, including our tolerance to a particular food, and whether it has, or appears to have, a good or adverse effect on us. Then there are current needs and requirements, likes and dislikes, which we ourselves have developed over time. In some cases these likes and dislikes may be fads or prejudices. If we like a particular food, we feel good after eating it. As far as Ayurveda is concerned, these responses are good ones, denoting that our body is happy with them. In the philosophy of Ayurveda, food is medicine for us, and has the task of maintaining the essential balancing of the *doshas* of *vata*, *pitta* and *kapha*.

In Ayurveda the six different tastes in food are the main help and test for us in our daily selection of food. Other characteristics are whether they are heavy or light, of an oily or wet nature, or dry. Another feature is hot or cold, not in the heat or fiery sense, but in the intimate and inherent nature of the food.

For example, pepper is hot in nature, and sugar is cold. Eggs are termed to be hot, and milk is cold. Wheat and meat are examples of being heavy, barley and chicken are light. Cheese is heavy and skimmed milk is light. Milk comes into the oily class, and so do beans and coconut. Dryness is contained in honey, cabbage and lentils. Hotness also includes pepper and honey while mint is cold in its character. Some foods possess more than one characteristic: milk, for an example, is a food both light and oily.

The main purpose is always to obtain and maintain a state of wellness in the individual. In India where Ayurveda is used widely, instead of allopathic medical practices, a twin-track approach is often required. The essential balancing of the three *doshas* is always the aim, and accomplished by the use of Ayurvedic drugs, which is only a stronger version of the balancing action normally obtained in the body from food. Drugs, however, will be more pronounced in their action and with almost immediate effect.

We come to the question, what is the best or correct diet for you? Having found out your dominant *doshas* according to the answers given in the questionnaire on your constitutional type (pages 14-25), you are in the position to proceed with the balancing act. The effect will be to reduce the energy or force of your dominant *dosha* and strengthen the other *doshas* or just one of the other *doshas* that needs fortifying, where this is found to be necessary. For example, there is a tendency for some people to over-develop the *kapha* type. In this situation it will be necessary to maintain the *kapha dosha*, with foods that will keep the *dosha* happy, or perhaps modify the *dosha* slightly and, at the same time, have foods that will strengthen the other two *doshas* of *pitta* and *vata*.

Often your body will give the signals needed to enable you to control your diet and intake of food. The knowledge is within us, but we have to release this and allow feeling and intuition to help us out, and to tell us that some adjustment is needed.

In Ayurveda, food is always looked upon as a natural therapy, not simply to keep us satisfied and in good health. The balanced diet in Ayurveda will normally contain all six tastes, or *rasa*, and there is an advantage in taking something daily of each of the tastes in our diet.

The quality of the food will affect the *doshas*. These qualities, or *gunas* in Ayurveda are: *sattva* (purity), *rajas* (energy or passion) and *tamas* (inertia, or heaviness). Ayurveda holds a position on vegetarianism and maintains that it is advisable to have a meatless diet. However, where this is not possible, a gradual lessening of the amount of meat taken can be tried, gradually reducing the amount of meat dishes eaten over a period. You will then be on the way to a meatless diet which is regarded as healthiest. This includes reducing red meat, that is beef, pork and veal, and replacing it with fish or chicken. Protein can be obtained from various beans and lentils for example, blackeye beans contain up to 25 per cent of their total weight in protein. Another good bean is the mung, or green bean. This bean is very much used in India, and is easily digested. Lentils are also a good form of food and protein and again form up to 25 per cent of total weight in protein. There are also a large number of other common foods containing a good proportion of protein, including the basic food of wheat.

With our knowledge of Ayurveda we are now taking hold of the whole subject of diet and especially the importance of the three *doshas*. With our existing knowledge and by gradually noting and observing the effect different items of food and diet have upon us, we will be able to build on a plan we ourselves draw up and which suits our special circumstances, bearing in mind the differences in constitution. Often the adjustment to food need only be small, and can easily be brought about. With the *dosha* classification for different foods, advantage is then taken of making any changes. These adjustments will then balance any of the *doshas*, righting the system and helping restore us to the condition of well-being.

2

The Constitution

We all differ in our constitutions, but they can be placed broadly into three main types. The need to find out the main constitution type for each individual is fundamental in Ayurveda. When this information is available, the mode to assist in the maintenance of health and, if necessary, the choice of treatment for a particular disease can be greatly enhanced.

A clear-cut and overwhelmingly one-type constitution under Ayurveda, or indeed under any other system, is quite rare. Most of us are made up of divisions containing the three main categories of constitution, and these types relate to the three *doshas*, that is *vata*, *pitta* and *kapha*. Doctors in Ayurveda will develop their own methods of identifying the type of constitution in each individual. This development may take doctors many years, and eventually evolve into a fine art. Lifestyle adjustments and diet requirements will be based on each constitutional type.

In finding out a person's main constitutional type, we are often able to pinpoint the predominant features of the three *doshas vata*, *pitta* and *kapha*, and make adjustments to live more closely within the individual calls and demands of the body. There are eight main types of constitution: these are *vata,pitta, kapha,* then *vata-pitta, pitta-vata, pitta-kapha* and *kapha-pitta.* Finally, you can have the *vata/pitta/kapha* type. It will be seen after you have completed the questionnaire on your own constitutional type (on pages 20–25) that it is uncommon for a person to belong to one type exclusively. In general, we usually have attributes from all three *doshas.* Fairly often, however, one particular *dosha* will tend to dominate, or at least will score the maximum points.

In general terms and from a psychological viewpoint, *vata* people have short memories but good mental powers, but are not too strong on willpower, tolerance, confidence, courage and boldness. They can also be rather irritable in temperament. *Pitta* people will have average memory and powers of reasoning. *Kapha* people will have strong memory but the grasp will not be too strong. They possess very good and strong willpower and, at the same time, are tolerant, confident and courageous.

The nature of digestion, appetite and other factors will also vary with each constitutional type individual. For *vata,* there can be poor appetite accompanied by poor digestion, lesser thirst, lesser sweat and sometimes disturbed sleep. In *pitta* people the appetite and the digestion are excellent. They will be able to eat a lot with no trouble at all, and possess a good general sleep pattern. *Kapha* people will possess moderate appetite and also moderate digestion. Their food intake can be less, and they enjoy good sound sleep and of quite long duration.

In the case of body build and other physical factors, *vata* people sometimes have an underdeveloped small frame, and their skin will tend to be dry. Hair can be dry, wavy and lacking lustre. For *pitta* people the body frame will be medium, complexion fair and smooth, hair tending to be rather thinner, but silky, and there can be some tendency to greyness. Lastly, the *kapha* individual generally has a well-developed body frame, the complexion is fairer or bright, with darker smooth hair, and prominent, bright eyes. From the Ayurveda texts there is much information and guidelines to enable the physician to gauge the possible constitution of an individual but this judgement will still rely on the physician's own experience and interpretation.

For many people the questionnaire (pages 20–25) will produce a double predominance in the case of two out of the three *doshas*. There are many possible permutations and results leading from this analysis, which brings home to us that the situation is almost infinite, and illustrates the truth in saying we are all different, and is yet more evidence to us of our own individuality.

Vata Constitution
Taking the three constitutional types in more detail, we firstly have *vata prakriti* (constitution). This *dosha* is made up of air and space, that is, air and vitality, or *prana*, and much in control of the total movement in the body. *Vata* can be described as being in charge or control, and these general characteristics link up with the person who is considered to have a *vata* constitution. Such a person will be very active, tending to be on the move all the time. He or she will be full of new ideas and have a measure of unpredictability that could border on the erratic or eccentric. A person of this type could suffer from erratic bowel movement, have a dry skin, which could in any event be rather thin and fragile. He or she would tend not to be very strong physically, but will walk and talk quickly, and in general be in a state of continual activity. Their minds can change rapidly as also do their moods. At night they will be able to sleep well when tired, but sometimes can remain sleepless. There is

also a tendency for inconsistency and unsteadiness, and for the mind and body to be rather restless. Where they are feeling on top of the world, they will talk a lot, can worry, and be thinking all the time of whatever they are interested in until that high level of energy is exhausted. Later, they will go out again and expend the newly stored-up energy. *Vata* seems to be at times an all or nothing affair. *Vata* people will tend to hurry through life, and even sometimes forget to say thank you during this hectic rushing about. They can suffer from wind, constipation and feeling cold, having cold hands and feet.

The very nature of *vata* and its dryness gives the general character to the *dosha*, of dryness and of moving quickly, in fact sometimes like the cold wind. *Vata* people will thus like light and also heat. This constitution as a whole is one difficult to control, because of its rapid deployment of matter and energy. *Vata* constitutions can sometimes digest the heaviest of meals, and at other times have indigestion, another sign of an unpredictable nature. Here we see again the importance of keeping to a diet where types of food taken will not vitiate or increase *vata dosha*. In general, oily and food-giving lubrication will in themselves relax and help the troubled *vata dosha*, so also will salty and spicy items.

Pitta Constitution
This *dosha*, comprising fire and water, is mainly concerned with heat and the digestive activities of the body. Thus the predominantly *pitta* person will give a strong impression of youthfulness, where he or she is in the teenage stage of life. *Pitta* types will be very intelligent, have a good memory, and probably be brave. They can become angry quickly, but will cool rapidly. With a powerful *pitta dosha*, *pitta* people will be in control of most situations, and be very logical.

Because of the strong *dosha*, normally their meals will be digested quickly and soon they will be hungry again. Although having a good appetite, they would usually be unable to carry out a lot of physical labour.

Pitta people are strong minded, like to eat and also to compete. They will tend to value regularity and could be classified as perfectionists. This aim for perfection has sometimes the effect of their being critical of others. Being a well-disciplined lot, their natural warmth will tend to create a sense of courage but, on the other hand, this very heat can produce anger, and will be at the basis of most of their discomfort and diseases.

Kapha Constitution
The last of the *doshas* is *kapha*, and the third part of the triangle. Being formed out of earth and water, it represents all that is calm, steady and stable. As a type *kapha* people tend to possess more weight, with eyes of blue, plenty of hair, and are generally slower moving than *vata* and *pitta* types. In a paradoxical sort of way, the real *kapha* type does not continually feel hungry but will keep to having regular meals. Any skipping of meals can, however, bring some mental discomfort as, although *kapha* people are and usually appear to be calm and placid, they are emotional underneath, with strong feelings. They never seem to be in a hurry, and will consider everything in life with care. The tendency is for them to take second place. In a command structure these folk will usually be in that position quite happily and will not have the spark of the *vata* person, or the intensity of *pitta* people. They are very respectful and will always form good and lasting friendships. Sometimes their easy ways will tend towards laziness, and sometimes they may need a push to get them into some sort of action again.

As the *kapha dosha* is located in the respiratory system, *kapha* people will have problems with stuffy noses, headaches, will not like cold water, and also not be fond of cold food. Stiff joints and joint pains are a feature which can be suffered so it is important to keep this *dosha* in balance along with the others, by way of balancing diet. Among the food especially liked by *kapha* constitutional-type people are fatty foods and sweet things. Included in the diseases which *kapha* over-balance or over-abundance can produce are those of asthma, coughs and metabolic conditions, such as diabetes, as well as problems brought about by overweight.

The Questionnaire
In Ayurveda it is important to find out to which constitution type we belong. Our basic constitution is fixed for us at the moment of conception, so we have those tendencies with us from our earliest days. In the present evaluation we will be checking and recording ourselves at this present time and not as we may need to alter for the future. We will almost certainly find that in Ayurveda and its system of diet, adjustments can be made to improve our state of wellness and health.

The system of classification helps in many ways and also explains a number of things. It will give guidance for a radical scheme of diet for the maintenance of health. It is worth knowing the main aspects of our own constitution, which will also be helpful in recognising constitutional aspects in other people.

The A, B, and C sections in this questionnaire relate to *vata*, *pitta* and *kapha* respectively. Where a question cannot be decided easily, or where you feel that you shift your position between the varying characteristics, it will be fairly safe to score yourself as *vata*. Questions found to be easier to answer are often those relating to physical characteristics.

1   YOUR BODY STRUCTURE AND WEIGHT
A   Short. Thin and wiry, often having difficulty in gaining weight but quite easily losing it.
B   Delicate, medium, plump, usually in good proportion.
C   Well proportioned, well built. Can gain weight easily, and has difficulty in losing it.

2   YOUR BODY FRAME
A   Lean, short, thin, irregular.
B   Medium, plump. Usually proportionate.
C   Well or heavily built. Well proportioned.

3   YOUR SKIN
A   Dry, rough, especially during the winter months. Often cold to the touch.
B   Soft, oily, marks, reddish, fair. Sweats easily. Warm to the touch.
C   Clear, glossy, fair, smooth, pale. Tans easily. Cool to the touch.

4   YOUR HAIR
A   Rather thin, dry.
B   Tendency to greying or balding, soft, thin, silky, fine, often straight.
C   Abundant, wavy, coarse, glossy. No early greying or falling out of hair.

5   BODY TEMPERATURE
A   Less than normal, often palms and feet are cold. Not liking cold weather and tolerates it badly. Sensitive to draughts.
B   Rather more than normal, palms, feet, face and forehead warm or hot. During hot weather, can feel uncomfortable, unwell and tired.
C   Normal, palms and feet cool.

6 YOUR JOINTS
A Protuberant.
B Loose, fairly well hidden.
C Strong, well knit, firm, well hidden.

7 YOUR BODY MOVEMENTS
A Unsteady with tendency to wander. Often a lot of movement of hands, legs, and shoulders.
B Quick, rapid.
C Slow, steady, unhurried.

8 YOUR VOICE
A Rough, weak, dry.
B Clear, loud, strong.
C Deep, pleasant, soft.

9 YOUR TALK
A Very talkative, fast, diffused speaking.
B Talkative, good speaker, good at arguments. Speaks purposefully.
C Slow, steady, firm but limited speech, cautious.

10 SWEATING
A Nothing very much, even in heat.
B Sweats easily.
C Not much sweating.

11 YOUR APPETITE AND THIRST
A Unpredictable, irregular and variable.
B Good, has to eat again after three or four hours, not liking hunger or thirst. Sometimes eats large quantities. Hates to miss a meal or having to eat late.
C Eats less when required, and can tolerate hunger and thirst. Can easily miss a meal with not too much discomfort.

12 QUANTITY OF FOOD AND DRINK TAKEN
A Not fixed at all, sometimes large, sometimes less.
B Can eat large quantities, comparatively more.
C Comparatively less.

13 WHAT KIND OF FOODS PREFERRED
A Hot and moist
B. Cold or warm, chilled, not too highly seasoned or too hot.
C Hot and dry.

14 EVACUATION
A Erratic. Often constipated.
B Loose, once or twice a day. Usually regular.
C Once a day. Regular, slow.

15 YOUR WORKING STRENGTH
A Limited, gets tired after only small amount of work. Tendency to over-exert.
B Moderate, tires after a limited amount or quality of work. Not keen on too much physical or mental exertion. Tendency to over-exert when competing.
C Good, and can do large amounts of work without feeling tired. Good energy level, remaining constant. Tendency to under-exert.

16 HOW YOU WORK
A Quickly, and in a hurry.
B. Medium or fast.
C Steadily, slowly, unhurriedly.

17 YOUR GRASPING AND UNDERSTANDING POWERS
A Sometimes quickly, but often finds some difficulty in learning and grasping. Often verbal.
B Always quickly, neatly, efficiently. Lots of visual imagery.

Rather slow in understanding. Much use of feelings and emotions. Usually grasping rather late but ultimately understanding well.

18 YOUR MEMORY CAPACITY

A   Forgets quickly. Difficulty in remembering things for long. Can learn quickly.

B   Moderate, can remember things well. Forgets only slowly.

C   Good long-term memory. Thoughtful. Learns slowly, forgets slowly.

19 SEXUAL DESIRE

A   Less. Variable.

B   Medium. Can be intense.

C   Abundant. Steady.

20 FERTILITY

A   Poor

B   Medium

C   Good

21 YOUR SLEEP

A   Often interrupted, and can be less than six hours. Deep when tired.

B   Needs six to eight hours. Sleeps easily, rises early.

C   Needs eight hours plus, sound. Takes time to wake up.

22 YOUR DIGESTION

A   Can be fairly easily upset. Prone to flatulence and constipation.

B   Regular, more prone to diarrhoea than constipation.

C   Regular, steady.

23 YOUR NATURE

A Lively, enthusiastic. Open to new ideas. Walks quickly and lightly. Talkative, speaks quickly. Moods can change quickly and according to feeling. Active mind, quick body movements. Sudden bursts of energy. Easily excited. Often worried and anxious.

B Medium strength, strong willed, precise, deliberate, short tempered, less patience, inclination to be perfectionist. Direct, not very tolerant, critical of self and others, self-respecting, brave, clever. Although not always showing it, often irritated or angry. Can be obstinate.

C Grateful, brave, good self-control, calm, placid, seldom angry, good at money problems, cheerful, gentle, constant staying power and energy. Walks slowly and deliberately. Eats slowly and with attention. Good memory, generous, thoughtful, stable.

24 HOW YOU TACKLE PROBLEMS

A Worries about them, anxious, difficulty in making decisions.

B Can make firm and good decisions quickly. Enjoys challenges and achieving goals.

C Takes good and right decisions calmly, but this can take time.

25 THINGS THAT ARE DIFFICULT TO COPE WITH OR TOLERATE

A Cold.

B Heat, hunger, thirst.

C Because of nature, can cope with and tolerate the majority of situations.

26 CLIMATE

A Prefers warm.

B Prefers cool.

C Likes the changes in seasons.

27 EMOTION

A Often fearful.

B Sometimes afflicted with anger.

C Aims to avoid argument and confrontation.

The results of this questionnaire will provide a way of focusing on various characteristics of our constitution. It is in no way meant to impose any limitations on us, nor to give us any type of label or restriction. Its use is as an aid to self-examination, self-development and self-knowledge. We are part of the world order, and in a greater context, a piece of the cosmos.

Answers sometimes can be within, say, three points of each other in the cases of two of the *doshas*. This result will indicate almost equal strength to both.

Examples of results:

	A	B	C	
	16	4	7	*Vata*
	4	15	8	*Pitta*
	8	5	14	*Kapha*
	12	11	5	*Vata–Pitta*
	9	12	6	*Pitta–Vata*
	10	8	9	*Vata–Pitta–Kapha*

3
The System

The Five Elements
The science of Ayurveda is based on the *panchamahabhoota*
theory, which is of the five elements. All is contained in this
theory, which includes the relationship of tissues, organs of
the body, diet, the *doshas*, and the essential links they have
with each other.

Firstly, there is earth, the solid state. Next there is water,
the liquid state. Then, thirdly, there is fire, the burning or
transforming force or state. Fourthly air, the gaseous state,
and lastly, the fifth, ether or space, which is simultaneously
the source of all matter and the space in which it exists (see
also page 34).

Doshas in Charge
The *doshas* are the controlling forces within the body and
influence the working of the tissues and the metabolic end
products, which is the *mala*. Being in charge, they are the
forces that makes the body tick.

The first thing to consider is the dynamic principle which
relates to the cell or first cell, which when impregnated will
begin to divide and gradually be organised through what
can be described as the inherent force. This force is the *vata*.

Not only is it concerned with the cell, or cells, but goes on to create the different structures of the body, including blood vessels and nerves. Later, this inherent force manifests itself into higher states, which can be classified as nerve force. It is interesting to note that in the ancient writings on Ayurveda the meaning of *vata* is given not as 'nerve force' but as 'cell force'.

The second *dosha* principle, *pitta* is the one which generates and maintains the heat of the body. It is concerned with metabolism, preparing the food and the nourishment that is to be absorbed into the body. The metabolism that controls the skin and the muscles is also under the control of the *pitta dosha*.

Lastly, we come to the third member of the *doshas*, the *kapha*. This is in essence the cooling and preservative principle in the body. This cooling procedure acts as a kind of water-cooling system as in the case of the internal combustion engine. The way it does this is by maintaining and giving out the normal secretions that are required by the body, so *kapha* is maintaining an important preservative function.

There is no ambiguity about the three *doshas* in the oldest texts on Ayurveda, which were compiled by Sushruta, Vagbhata and Charaka, and nothing has been added today. In summarising the *doshas*, we can describe *vata* as the force that upholds the constituents of the body and determines their path through the body. Then there is the *pitta* whose principal characteristic is its metabolic function and digestion, the faculty of vision, and the regulation of temperature. Overall it represents, so to speak, the fire of the body. *Kapha* represents the cooling systems of the body, with oily secretions and preservative functions. It also generates strength, growth, courage and virility.

The Dhatus

These costitute the second platform in Ayurveda, the science of life. The *dhatus*, or tissues, are created and nourished in the first place by the food we eat. Here we see how significant is the role of food in relation to health in Ayurveda.

The tissues, or *dhatus*, are made up of the five elements or categories, which give the different types of tissues their individuality and properties. Again we see that in these elements, some contain more *agni* or fire, and assist in carrying out reactions in the body. Then there are those where the principal job is to stay calm and collected.

Doshas are in control of the *dhatus*, giving them orders, for the *dhatus* cannot act or perform on their own. However, the *doshas* in their turn help to renew the tissues, so there is a continued interaction going on in our bodies. In this spirit of co-operation between the *dhatus* and the *doshas*, we have a situation where the food is assimilated, forming and replacing the tissues and, at the same time, the *doshas* themselves very much influence the functions and working of the tissues.

Tissues in Ayurveda are divided into seven different types, the first of which is *rasa*. Food well digested by us is called *sara*, and the product and fluid formed from our food is that which nourishes the main tissues in this division of Ayurveda and will be recognised by us as being the plasma or extracellular fluid of the human body. It is interesting here to note that the word *ras* itself is Sanskrit, meaning 'to move'. This is exactly what is happening as *ras* in effect is the body's sap. *Rasa* comes within the *dosha kapha*, so that this *dosha* is important to *rasa*, and greatly influences its properties. This number one in the main division of tissues *rasadhatu*, influences the rest of the six divisions of tissues.

Tissues coming second in the Ayurveda order of importance

is *raktadhatu*, the blood, which relates to both red and white blood cells. This division comes under the *pitta dosha*, so the basic elements are fire and water. One of the essential tasks of *raktadhatu* is to bathe the flesh and the muscles.

The third division is *mamsadhatu*, which relates to the skin and ligaments. This will primarily interact with the *kapha dosha*, so it is of the earth element.

The next in line in the classification of tissue matter is *medadhatu*, or fat tissue. This is of the elements earth and water, and is strongly linked with *kapha dosha*, and especially to the *kapha diet*. The main job of fat is to oil or lubricate the system. A by-product of this is the act of sweating or excessive sweating, which is sometimes a problem. Part of sweat is grease and people of heavy weight sometimes appear to have a greasy skin.

The next tissue is *asthidhatu*, or bone, which is very much in touch with *vata* of the *doshas*. Other secondary tissues in this classification are the teeth. The so-called waste, or by-products of *asthidhatu* are hair and nails.

The sixth classification is *majjadhatu*; this includes the bone marrow and nervous tissue. Having water as the main element, the tissue will be relying largely upon *kapha* for its main course of instruction.

Lastly, we have the tissue classification of *shukradhatu*, representing a very important part of our physical make-up, that is the seed, the sperm and egg; its overall function will reflect sexual urges and procreative functions.

From the description of the different types of tissues, it is seen that every one of them is well ordered and stable, and are all influenced by environmental situations and conditions. The *doshas* play an essential and dynamic part in all this, always changing and adjusting, helping in one tissue after another, transforming, having the job of maintaining all in harmony, and giving us a sense of well-being or wellness.

Mala

The waste products of the body, called *mala*, are in a more formal way metabolic end-products, and include more than the familiar urine and faeces. Ayurveda affords them the status of importance for the proper functioning of the body and in maintaining the health of the individual.

However, there is rather more to *mala*. This is because each cell in the body is, of course, a living thing, and under the control of our *doshas* will produce chemicals which influence the tissues that produce them in the first place. We now begin to realise the importance of *mala* within this amazing constructive communication within our own bodies.

Srotas, Cells and Tissues

There is always a great deal of communicating going on within our bodies, and scientists already know a lot about this continual signalling within ourselves. Ayurveda says that this communication goes on within channels, both macro and micro, called *srotas*. Each of the seven major classification of tissues has its own set-up of communication channels. These channels are not just inactive conduits but form a participatory function of the tissues they serve. *Srotas* have a major receptive role in the function of the cell, and anything going wrong in their proper functioning can have serious consequences for the cell and the tissue.

In Ayurveda, the Sanskrit word *srota* meaning 'channels', also means the whole internal transport system of the cells in the body.

The substances which nourish the tissues are made available to them through their own specific *srota*. The relevant *srota*, relating to the different tissues in the body, have in them a natural discrimination as to what kind of nutrients should be made available to the tissues. Similarly, the tissues themselves also possess this discriminatory feature of knowing what kind of nutrients they need. So there is a two-way system in operation which again demonstrates the absolute co-operation existing in the human body under normal circumstances.

The cell (*dhatu*) is the smallest functional unit in the body, and Ayurveda lists seven different types of tissues. These cells together form the organs, which make up the whole body. For quite a while modern medicine has realised that the individual cell is the functional unit of the body, and it is interesting to note that Ayurveda recorded and recognised this fact long ago. The importance of balancing the *doshas* has already been mentioned, as without this proper balance, the state of the tissues involving both *doshas* and tissues leads to disease. Where these are balanced there is a state of health and well-being. Having a good quality in tissues is then of great importance in Ayurveda. For a disease to occur, some malfunction in the cell will have to happen and a weakness in the cell will make it prone to external and internal stresses.

The Time of Your Life
During a person's life, in general terms, childhood is the time when *kapha* has the upper hand, while in teenagers and young adults, *pitta* will tend to be the stronger force. Later, *pitta* gives way to *vata*. The position day to day, is that the morning is the *kapha* part, and this being the case, one would be wise to avoid too heavy a breakfast, and to do some exercise, even it is only just walking. In the after-noon, *pitta* is beginning to build up its force. Thus it would be good to have a full meal, but such a meal should not

normally be left until too late into the evening. It is in the evening that the *dosha vata* will be starting to build up.

Weather and Seasons

We come to consider the way in which the four seasons can affect the *doshas* in ourselves. Usually, in the changing of the seasons, they are in themselves part of a fairly gradual progress, so that here we are not looking for, and will not receive, any sudden or violent change to our body pattern. In considering the effect the seasons have on ourselves, Ayurveda will have in mind the variations that we can make in our diet to counterbalance these changes on the *doshas*. Starting with spring, nature is stirring, the plants are budding and the whole world is beginning to come into a new cycle of life. In the prelude to spring, we have been coping with the effects of colder weather. Over the past decade or so, the harsher winter conditions experienced previously do not now appear to be happening in the UK, at least not as they occurred in the past. There is no doubt that the general weather patterns throughout the world appear to be changing. According to the experts, there has been some increase in the average temperature worldwide, which in itself has led to the changes in weather patterns.

During the year, there will be variations in the activity pattern of the *doshas*. In the winter we will have favoured food of a warming and heating nature. Hot meals, and occasional hot drinks, would have been on the menu; in other words, food that generates heat in the body will have been preferred. Bearing in mind the sensible need for hot meals and drinks during this time, generally the *doshas* should have been in good order, but perhaps in the winter months of January and February they would have needed some extra care and attention. In summer there can be a build-up with *vata dosha* becoming dominant, so extra care is again needed during those summer months, especially where we come into some really hot or thundery weather. The *dosha pitta* is strong in the latter part of summer and also in the autumn. The *doshas* are really unsettled, or can become unsettled, in changeable and unsettled weather. We have all experienced feeling rather uncomfortable in those sorts of conditions.

In really hot weather, the need to control *dosha vata* will be strong, so sweet, sour, and salty items of food which will not affect *vata* can be taken, keeping away from bitter and astringent foods as they will increase the *vata dosha*. Many vegetables, including carrots, turnips, cauliflowers are good and useful items to include in the diet at this time. Foods having quite a high carbohydrate content can be eaten, as these will not affect *vata*. Items such as milk, and milk products, can be taken in controlled quantities only, because they are heavier types of food, and later will require more work by the digestive system. During the past decade or so, we have not been experiencing marked contrasts in the four seasons of the year, so that the *doshas*, although certainly affected by climatic conditions, will not be greatly disturbed during the seasonal variations.

Ayurveda says that there is a certain pattern, a rhythm, in everything in the natural world and this certainly does not exclude us human beings. Not only the famous three, the three *doshas*, change in their importance and dominant position throughout the life of each person, but also this principle will be applied to every year, every month, every season, every day, and in fact every moment of our lives. We are changing all the time.

We Are What We Eat
We have heard people say 'we are what we eat'. In Ayurveda,

this is a fundamental truth. Diet alone, however, is not considered to be the ultimate solution to everything concerning health, but rather diet is always considered in direct relationship to the person, the eater. Therefore, what is fundamentally important in Ayurveda is not only the diet of a person but also the 'internal' processing of food, so keeping the *doshas vata, pitta* and *kapha* in balance.

Elements in Food
Ayurveda gives diet to contain, as in all things in the universe, the five elements of earth, air, fire, space and water. All food is affected by the proportions of elements it contains. For example, where an item of food contains a good proportion of element earth (not of course earth or soil itself), that is, bulk or material substance, then this will increase *kapha dosha*. Where there is more of the fire (*agni*) element, the digestive and metabolic processes will be in very good order. However, if the diet contains a good proportion of *vata* or space, in itself it will be easy to digest and will help to reduce body weight. Many items of food will contain more than one factor affecting the three *doshas*, so that this has also to be taken into account.

Importance of Tastes
Our food and diet will have six tastes which will in themselves have their own properties and values according to the elements earth, fire, water, space and air. They are the values of: sweet, sour, salty, bitter, pungent and astringent. Each of these tastes have their own peculiarities.

Varying Diet
It is a wise policy for us to vary our daily set of meals, so as to include something representing the six different tastes.

A balanced diet on Ayurvedic lines will contain at least something from each of the six tastes. Where we do this, then later we will be a in a position to cover the many-sided aspects of Ayurveda. For example. take the case of a rigid slimming diet containing mostly salad. Such food in itself is a good and healthy item of nutrition, but without care can lead to some constipation, where there is not sufficient lubrication in the diet. Such a tendency can easily be counteracted by including a little vegetable oil or clarified butter (*ghee*) in the salad diet.

Enjoy the Meal
The eating and production of the various constituents in a Ayurveda meal can be likened to a work of art. Later, when experience has been gained in Ayurveda, not only will the preparation and eating of the meal generally follow the principal rules, but the individual's intuition can be brought into play. The factors considered will first of all be the constitution of the person.

Differences however may only deviate in a person to a small degree. However, these differences need be taken into account. Where a person's constitution is mainly of the *vata* type, then it is best to avoid too many dry and light items of food and, instead, to have food that is oily, sweet, sour and salty. Where *pitta* is the main attribute in the constitution, then that person should take cold items having bitter, sweet and astringent tastes. The *kapha* person, the earth and water person, will need to take in hot and spicy food.

Cooking and Preparation
Cooking of food will include roasting, frying and garnishing during or after its preparation and cooking. A mention should be made of the addition of *vaghar*, which is regularly

used in Indian cooking and is a process whereby there is the addition of, say, mustard seed, methi and asafoetida (*hing*), all three of which are cooked in a vegetable oil, or clarified butter (*ghee*), for a few minutes and then added to the vegetables, the main course, or to the soup or stew. This has the effect of neutralising the food and affecting the *doshas vata*, *pitta* and *kapha*. Here again we see the effect of combining spices and other items in the preparation of food.

In Ayurveda the quantity of food should always be kept to a minimum. Again, the type of constitution of each person will be taken into consideration, so that the *pitta* person will need *kapha*, increasing items such as wheat products. The *kapha*-dominated person should be given plenty of vegetables in the diet.

Time to Eat

There are best or correct times and situations to eat, but of course, in busy periods, keeping to strict times may not always be easy. However keeping to a sensible breakfast routine is usually possible, and also the time and place when the main food of the day is taken. Often this will be in the evening. Ayurveda says that a person should, wherever possible, be in a good and relaxed frame of mind while eating as the food will then be well digested. We have perhaps only been too aware of situations when we have not been in a happy state, or when the food had to be eaten in a hurry. These situations can often be forced on us, but at least we know that they should be avoided whenever possible.

Mixing It

In Ayurveda certain items of food just do not mix or, put in another way, should not be taken together or at the same time. Such items include milk or milk products with fruit, meat or fish. The importance of quantity as well as quality of food in Ayurveda has already been stressed, and quantity should always be kept to a minimum.

Order of Eating
The conventions of eating food in a particular order have been well worked out for us over a long period. Ayurveda stresses the importance of attempting to quiet everything down, so that we are able to balance the three *doshas* in our favour. In the chapter setting out the effects on *doshas* of the various foodstuffs available to us today (page 64), it is seen that the same food can have increasing or subduing effects on more than one *dosha*. For example, the common item of milk produces *kapha* and at the same time subdues *pitta* and *vata*. The dual effect of many foodstuffs has to be taken into consideration when following our way to health through Ayurveda.

Lifestyle
We are looking at ways in which affect food and diet our health. Life has a limited span, and this is accepted, but we can and will be able to do something about increasing the quality. We would like several extra years added on to our life but at the same time we realise that the quality of life needs to be maintained to our satisfaction. The aim of Ayurveda is to achieve and maintain this quality.

Life before Birth
Ayurveda says that the earlier we are able to adopt a healthy lifestyle the better, and that we cannot be too young to start. It will be no surprise to see Ayurveda describing in some detail the measures parents can take even before a child is born, whereby the child has then a good chance of

remaining healthy for the rest of its life. So the concern at all times is centred on the effects diet has on health, even before birth.

Diet in pregnancy has been given special emphasis in Ayurveda which says that, during the first three months, the diet should be good and wholesome, which is common sense anyway. In the first three months, therefore, when the organs are forming, there is no special diet put forward, except to say that it be a wholesome one, accompanied by a moderate amount of exercise. The fourth month sees the formation of plasma, so the diet will have this target in view; the fifth month of blood and tissues, calling for nutritious foods. In the sixth month, all the organs will be formed, also the skin and hair, so that substances that will encourage growth of these tissues are good. The remainder of the pregnancy will need a diet to prevent constipation.

Maturing

In ageing, which can start at an earlier age than sixty-five, Ayurveda puts the blame fairly on the not-so-good *agni*, the digestive fire and processes of digestion. This means not being able to fully digest our food in the manner we were able to at a earlier age. The other problem is that the *vata dosha* has been vitiated, becoming faulty and not working at its full efficiency. The way out of this impasse is to pay special attention to factors strengthening our digestion through diet. We need better control of *vata dosha*, being careful to aim for reducing the wear and tear on our tissues, making sure that any specific illness or disease is treated and looked into as soon as possible.

Bearing in mind the not-so-strong *vata dosha*, heavy meals should be avoided as much as possible, instead of which smaller and lighter meals at regular times should take their place. Heavy meals at night and meals taken too late at night will make things difficult. Salty and sour items can be eaten with safety and will help control *vata*. Sweet items will also help with providing energy to the body. Milk is also very good, and can be relied upon in older age, as much as it did during our childhood. Sometimes milk taken where the *agni* is not up to full standard will not be digested easily and, to help this, a half of teaspoonful of dry ginger powder can be added to the milk. Constipation is another problem in old age, and here the plentiful eating of fruit and vegetables will help.

In Ayurveda, with its base in ancient history and philosophy, there is the important concept of realising and understanding the carrying out a good, clean lifestyle. From a practical point of view, this means taken care in our dietary procedures and disciplines, and especially in relation to bowel care, personal hygiene and relationships with other people.

At this stage in our evolution, so far no one has come up with the magic drug, the magic formula, to cure all diseases. We are still awaiting the cure-all, the magic bullet from Western medical practice and allopathy. It is possible that this goal may yet be a long way off. Ayurveda helps in the process of avoiding the need for a magic bullet.

Always Prevention
Ayurveda is primarily concerned with prevention, and rightly so. What is the point of curing a so-called disease with allopathic drugs when, because of lifestyle and diet, the disease or violation of the human system will continue, or return at some time in the future? In this sense, the system and philosophy of Ayurveda will win in the end. Can you imagine a human body gone or going wrong because of in-

correct lifestyle or diet, but maintained alive by a so-called wonder drug? It is already happening. What is the point in following that path?

Drugs and Diet

Drugs in Ayurveda are considered variations of diet, and are themselves obtained from natural sources and therefore merely an extension in a person's diet. There are literally hundreds of different medicinal plants used in Ayurveda, and their power and variety is extraordinary. In fact it is possible that there may not be a single herb in the world which is not medically useful or rich in some way.

Bitter is Good

It is interesting to find that many of the health-promoting drugs in Ayurveda are also the ones that have a bitter taste, as are the bitter-taste food items. It is the same in Western medicine: the effect of this bitter-tasting drug or diet will be to stimulate the appetite, reducing thirst, reducing fat, slow down watery conditions nasally, help in the purge of the intestine and against skin disorders. As far as the *doshas* are concerned, Ayurvedic drugs and diet items with the bitter taste will increase *vata*, and help with digestion.

The Whole Person

The strength of Ayurveda is not only in its role of delivering drugs and cures for numerous diseases and conditions, but also in its fundamental concern for caring for the whole person and its holistic attitude to people's health and well-being. We realise there is more to health than diet alone, but diet does and will play an essential role. Ayurveda poses the question – do we feel well? And are we in what is aptly described as being in a state of wellness?

We not only wish to keep free of diseases, but we also want to feel well all or at least most of the time. Today we are meeting a changing and ever-challenging environment, and facing new situations in the way we live, how we travel, how we work, and in our working conditions. All these variables and continual movements can pose problems for ourselves and the *doshas*. Fortunately, we can bring influence to bear on the provision of our own diet, and how and what we eat, and when we eat it.

The ancient writers on Ayurveda, Vaghbhata, Charaka and Sushruta would have had different times and different situations to deal with, but no doubt would have been equal to the task, if they had been presented with the conditions of today. In Ayurveda, there is *agnimandya*, meaning a condition brought about by weak digestion, a weak or faulty *agni* or fire of life, in other words, the digestion and its processes. In this condition, the meals eaten are not converted properly by the system into the essential nutriments and remain 'uncooked', or unprocessed, in the system. The body system does not like a situation where food is not converted properly into *rasa* nutrients, and is thereby not contributing to the maintenance and the creation of healthy tissues. The whole body metabolism can go wrong.

The Very Important Lady Agni
In Ayurveda, a person having or suffering from a faulty digestive system, in a bad temper, should avoid cold foods and those of a heavy or oily nature, and also avoid cold drinks. Vegetables such as onions, potatoes, peas, tomatoes, bananas pickles, all fried, hot in flavour, and spicy foods are not recommended. On the other hand, ginger and

garlic are good for the digestion and in stoking the digestive system. Ayurveda is concerned not only with quality
and the right kind of diet, eaten at the right time, but also
makes clear that the quantity of food we eat should also be
controlled and modified, according to the conditions at the
time. If not, the *agni*, the digestion, will rebel in being
taxed or strained to the limit. It can also happen that eating
specific foodstuffs will cause indigestion. For example, if
we have been eating an abnormal amount of sweet things,
such as confectionery and the like, the odds are that the
dosha kapha will rebel against the excess, and leave us feeling
heavy and lethargic. In such a case, a drastic cut down or
fasting will usually be the answer. In Ayurveda, the taking
of *soonth* (dried ginger powder) in warm water will help –
ginger is such an excellent food. Honey is another wonderful
food and its virtues are well known. It will help reduce the
fat content in the body, and at the same time be good for
the digestion. Honey also has high healing properties, and
is used in Ayurveda for dressing cuts and wounds. Garlic is
another well-known vegetable and good for the prevention
of coughs, colds and the reduction of gas formation in the
digestive system. It also has many other medicinal virtues,
including the lowering of the cholesterol level in the body.

Fasting or Cutting Down
The practice of fasting is an important part of keeping well
and assumes a high level of priority in the Indian subcontinent. The basic idea behind fasting, which can be carried
out on a regular basis, is to keep the gut clean and make
sure that digestion is complete. Taken during the partial
fast will be some vegetable oil, *ghee* (clarified butter) with
milk, and some roughage, such as green vegetables. If
taken in properly measured quantities, *ghee* does not

increase the much-talked-about cholesterol, instead it benefits in its function of being a most excellent food and nutrient. It will have the effect of giving valuable lubrication to the blood vessels, and also has many other good effects, all of which will help in one's ageing process.

4

Agni – *the Fire*

The driving force in our body, *agni* has been aptly described as the fire of life. Charaka said that *agni* is responsible for life, the body, tissues, strength and complexion of a person. As the sun is the force upon earth, so is *agni* the driving force of life inside the body. Again, *agni* influences the strength of tissues, and especially cells that are involved with immunity and the complexion of the skin.

In Ayurveda there are three classifications of *agni*: those resident in the stomach, the tissues and in the cells making up the tissues. There are, as is often the case in Ayurveda, sub-divisions of the three types. Of the main divisions *jatharagni* is the main *agni* concerned with stomach and digestion, and the most important one of the three. When it is working properly, all is well in the other two main divisions, which are *dhatvagni*, that relating to the tissues, and *panchabhootagni*, that which relates intracellularly in the elements that form the issues.

Ayurveda lays down the first principle saying that if all is well in the digestive department of our bodies, then we are on the way to well-being. When all is right in this division and our food gets completely digested, *sara*, the vital nutrient is properly obtained to supply the tissues. In this state, a person feels good. The main division of *agni* works in close co-operation with *dosha pitta*.

Occasionally, *agni* will go wrong and become unbalanced, and in such conditions, the result can be that the *dosha kapha* takes over and inserts its slow and contented pace to the *agni*, leading to a position that food will tend not to be properly digested. You can then have a situation of having uncooked or, as it were, unripe fruit in our bodies. What will also upset the functioning is overeating, or having too many snacks between meals. Here the digestive functions will not have completed their first and essential tasks, before more food to be digested arrives on the scene.

Factors affecting the digestion are many and include the quality and quantity of food, whether it is unhealthy food or too much or too little food, or taken at the wrong times or taken too many times each day, or too little taken each time. There are many variations.

Agni being the power and fire in digestion, it is essential to take account of its power in the maintenance of good health and wellness. We need to be careful as to what demands are made on our digestive system. The easier work we can give it, the better it will be pleased. Our digestive system will usually deal with all manner of work and situations. Overstraining the system will weaken the strength and the intensity of the *agni*. For example, it is usually not a good idea to have too late or large a meal at night, at which time it is too close to bedtime.

Our digestive system is given the job of digesting and possessing food given to it, and after this processing has taken place, the end product will be there to nourish the body. Ayurveda helps us towards giving the body this nourishment, and at the same time avoiding a situation of developing *ama*, the unwanted waste products caused by a faulty diet over a period of time.

An *ama* situation is similar to one in which we add an uncooked quantity of food to already uncooked ingredients. This can be a recipe for disaster, especially when there is a variety of different foods offered, and yet we tend to inflict this situation upon our stomach and digestive system time and time again.

Similarly, *agni* can get out of hand with an excessive or unbalanced *pitta dosha*. Here the digestive system will be working overtime, with the consequence that food to be digested is done so too quickly; in other words, food becomes 'burnt'. The person is left with a feeling of great hunger and eats at unbalanced and irregular times. This condition can lead to serious digestive conditions and diseases, including ulcers and gastric problems. Similarly, where the *dosha vata* goes haywire, cramp, colicky pain and constipation can result. Where the main *agni* relating to the digestive system becomes unbalanced, it can lead to a general weakness and a lessening of normal metabolism.

Agni then is the fire of life, and we have considered its three classifications. When this main classification of *agni*, *jatharagni*, goes wrong and it seriously misbehaves, we are in deep trouble, for our food, instead of getting converted into the main nutriment *sara*, is not properly converted at all. Our food can then become *ama*, evoking a strong immuneresponse as it is foreign to the body.

Good *agni*, the fire of digestion in us, is essential in Ayurveda. This fire should continue to burn throughout our life, burning brightly when we are in a state of well-being. At different times, in different people with varying constitutional types, the demands made on the digestive system are bound to differ. Ayurveda brings to us knowledge of the *doshas* and the other factors concerning the maintenance of health and the paths leading to this goal.

In Ayurveda, physicians, or *vaids* (being different from their surgeons), use a branch of medicine called *kayachikitsa*. *Kaya* is derived from the root word 'body', and this is what the body in its sum total represents, that is, made up of the food eaten, digested and assimilated. *Kayachikitsa* is Ayurveda treatment for the body, where digestion and proper assimilation of food have gone wrong. Ayurveda arrives at the position in stating that as the body and its functions result from the food we eat, nearly all diseases can be placed at the door of improper utilisation of food, our fuel, and the burning and digestion of it. The burning of the fuel or food is none other than *agni*.

Charaka said in a verse that 'the balance and aggravation of the *doshas* is at all times due to the relative strength or weakness of the digestive fire. Therefore the digestive fire must always be protected, and to prohibit all activities which might weaken it.'

The digestive system will be normal when there is a healthy need and desire for food, and no discomfort after a meal, with no uneasiness or feeling of heaviness and unease. On the other hand, there should be a sense of wellness or well-being, indicating that proper nourishment is being obtained for *rasa* (taste), and that all wastes are normal, bowel movement normal and occurring at the proper times.

We are saying that we should be avoiding overeating at all costs, and following the Ayurveda basic rule, which is to allow our digestive system the first meal, before we are unkind enough to give it another, so making the system start work all over again. There is little point in overeating one day, realising the strain that we have inflicted on our system, belatedly repenting a little, and the following day taking much less food or no food at all. But, in controlled eating, having much less food, or fasting, is a way of getting rid of undigested food (*ama*) in the system (see page 46).

After a therapeutic or Ayurveda fast, the *agni* in a person will again resume working in a normal fashion, and we will know and realise that this has happened; there is that regained sense of wellness. What can be said at this stage, however, is that after a fast, we should go back on to our diet in a gradual way, eating light foods in the first place. Our digestive system will need stimulating. In other words, our *agni*, the fire, requires that extra help we are able to give it.

By now we are beginning to understand the essential importance of diet in Ayurveda for the therapy and cure of disease. The first aim is towards a realisation that we must improve the digestion (the *agni*) and avoid *ama* (undigested food). The early warning signs that all is not well in the formation of *ama* are similar to that of indigestion. *Ama* then is the enemy from within and must be avoided at all costs.

Changes are occurring all the time relating to the body's digestive fire and these changes have to be dealt with. There are problems, for instance in the case of cold or liquid substances taken at incorrect times, especially during the winter, when over or under-eating can occur with too much heavy food also, and when insufficient time is allowed between meals and incorrect food combinations are forgotten. Other factors include: eating unfamiliar food, changes in climate, age, before or after over-activity, and also before and after under-activity. There may also be mental causes or conditions which will include: envy, greed, fear, anger, anguish, misery and sorrow.

The body, being the amazing mechanism it is, tries to deal

with the enemy *ama*, the undigested substances, in giving the body help by eliciting immune reactions.

There is a tendency in developed countries, with a higher standard of living, for people to suffer from health problems caused by or related to an over-consumption of protein, much of which comes from animal sources. These types of foods can have a habit of becoming stagnant in the intestines, with resultant encouragement of putrefactive bacteria, which convert the ingested food into the enemy *ama*.

Charaka compares the process to an agricultural system, in which good seeds sown at the proper time in the correct season in a well-tilled and well-watered field will invariably produce good crops. So it is in the human system: where food and diet are wholesome and correct in quality and combination, they will invariably produce good results.

Where food and diet are not right, in relation to the different factors and conditions occurring day by day, monthly, yearly, according to age and digestive power, then there can be problems. Particularly pronounced problems can occur during unsettled weather conditions, during the periods between different seasons, for example, between winter and spring and autumn into winter.

Where the fuel and the fire are not up to standard, we are in trouble and the enemy *ama* can be the result. The basic building blocks of *ama*, the molecules, become absorbed and cause serious disruption within the body. The variety of diseases resulting are endless, ranging from diarrhoea to chronic rheumatoid arthritis, diabetes and anaemia.

As *ama* is the later formation of intermediate products of digestion which have toxic properties and are in reality kinds of foreign compounds in the body, they will be treated as such by the body, which will counter-attack with anti-bodies created by the defence cells of the body.

In Ayurveda there is *prajnaparadha*, which is Sanskrit for 'perversity of mind'. This is mental *ama*, when the mind is unable to think correctly, leading to wrong sense perceptions, thoughts and emotions. Then there are incorrect or selfish thoughts that will affect the body, and will in turn disturb the consciousness. Therefore the fundamental cause of all *ama* is incorrect or indigestible desire.

So Ayurveda goes further than just considering *ama* as dietary indiscretions; it lays down firmly that emotional stress, such as grief, worry and fear, can contribute to its formation. These factors are not the only ones present when considering the question of health and disease. Others come into play, such as subtle genetic defects bringing about changes in proteins and enzymes, lack of proper dietary constitutes, defective penetration of essential nutrients into the cells of the body – all these can interfere with the proper functioning of the cells. Diagnosis in the science of Ayurveda relies heavily on any abnormality at cellular level, and is described therefore as the gross manifestations that will be present, and not by lengthy investigations or investigative methods. This diagnosis will also include knowledge as to what stage the disease has arrived at, and what information can be ascertained by the different symptoms evident at its different stages.

When *ama* is formed and distributed in this way, it will block the channels (*srotas*) in the body. This will have the effect of upsetting proper communication within the body, and the *vata dosha* will become out of order. In the early stages, there will be warning signs such as nausea and vomiting. A lot of information is nowadays available to us on how the body and our digestive system deals with food and, although the question and existence of *ama* from a nutritional point of view may be relatively unimportant, from the body's immunological viewpoint, it is extremely important and powerful, as this condition comes about as the result of improperly digested food. Hence the body system is called upon to attempt a great deal of extra work.

This improperly digested food imposes a strain on our system, and the body, being the wonderful machine and work of art that it is, will set in motion the formation of antibodies by the defence cells in the body. The *ama* and the antibodies will then interact with each other and form an immune complex which can result in serious problems, such as an inflammatory reaction as blood cells mount an attack, not only killing bacteria, which is their primary purpose, but also inflicting serious damage to tissues. In the joints, for example, this total action can result in destroying normal tissue, leading to much pain and a swelling, as in the case of arthritis.

In Ayurveda, the problem can be approached in a three-part way: if *ama* is already formed, medicines and dietary items will be given to digest the *ama*; another plan is to remove it physically through vomiting or purging. Thirdly, when the *ama* has already been absorbed into the system and is of long-standing duration, then drugs will be given to strengthen the tissues affected, and help them to stand up to the problems and to attack the *ama* deposits.

5
Tastes

In Ayurveda, there is the need to draw a balance between different elements of the three *doshas* in our own bodies and to maintain a proper balance in the body chemistry. Given an overall knowledge of Ayurveda and awareness of the vital importance of the three *doshas*, we find a way of putting this science of life into practice. One of the main ways, and probably an obvious one, is the taste of our food. Different foods with their different properties will increase, stimulate or subdue the quality and action of any one or more of the three *doshas*: *vata*, *pitta* and *kapha*.

We are not food laboratories, having the facility to analyse each type of food, but there is the vital sense of *rasa* (taste), at our disposal, which provides the key enabling us to deal with all our food. Each element or type of food has a characteristic taste, and with this knowledge and understanding we are able to deal with each *dosha* on an individual basis.

The different tastes, as we have already seen, are divided into six main categories: sweet, sour, pungent, bitter, salty and astringent. Each of these tastes represents a combination of two elements, the *tattwas*. Firstly, the sweet taste is a combination of water and earth elements and a pure example of this group is sugar. Next there is the sour taste and again, as far as the elements are concerned, will represent a mixture of earth and fire. Lemon and vinegar are examples. Following on is the pungent taste, and this is formed by air and fire. Peppers and pickles are in this group. The bitter taste comes next, produced by a combination of air and ether. Bitter lemon is an example and so is quinine. A very pronounced taste comes next, the salty one, and is contained within the elements of water and fire; plain table salt is the example that immediately comes to mind. Lastly, is the astringent taste, a combination of air and earth. Alum is a representative of this group, and honey also comes into this category, although honey is both sweet and astringent.

With these six tastes and our knowledge of the *doshas* included in all foods, we are able to operate and balance the three to our own needs and advantage. As far as taste and the *doshas* are concerned, food combinations act directly on the three *doshas* in the following way:

Vata: this is stimulated by astringent, bitter and pungent tastes and subdued by sweet, sour and salty tastes.
Pitta: affected and stimulated by pungent, sour and salty tastes and subdued by sweet, astringent and bitter tastes.
Kapha: stimulated by sweet, sour and salty tastes, and subdued by bitter, pungent and astringent tastes.

Firstly, we have the sweet items of food (*madhur rasa*). Food containing sweetness will have in itself the elements of water and earth, coming under the *dosha kapha*. These foods are necessary for the maintenance of the body and the repair of tissues. There is, however, a tendency for the production of fatty tissue, but this can be avoided if a proper mix of diet is taken. In sweet items of diet, there can be a much quieter *agni*, or fire, in our digestive system, which can lead to excess *kapha* giving us some lethargy. Along with this general feeling, a pronounced surplus of *kapha*-producing items in the diet can lead to colds and coughs, nausea, vomiting, high blood pressure and being overweight. There are numerous items in our diet that are not sweet but are *kapha*, for example, fruit, milk and milk products, eggs, fish and meat – all containing a lot of water as an element, but not necessarily tasting sweet. In Ayurveda, it is the *rasa*, or taste, that is produced after the food has been processed in the digestive system, which is the *sara* – the well-digested food. It is this, *the rasahatu*, which will influence the quality of the three *doshas*.

Examples of the sweet taste are grains, such as wheat and oats; oranges and bananas; vegetables including onions and cabbage; lentils and peas; walnuts and peanuts. For the oils, these will include sunflower and olive oil, sweet dairy items including milk, butter and *ghee*, meat, potatoes and, of course, sugar. There is a great variety of sweet items to choose from, and this list is not an exclusive one.

Next are the sour items of diet (*amla rasa*), containing earth and fire under the Ayurvedic classification. The fire in this will increase *agni*. This taste is not by any means as common or widespread as som other tastes in the group but, in some circumstances, a sour taste will tend to dispel a feeling of nausea from occurring, which in itself can be very helpful. Sour items will help keep *vata dosha* under control and well balanced. On the other hand, too many sour items of food will increase the *dosha pitta*, that is, fire and water. Limes, citrus fruits, tomatoes, lemon, vinegar, dairy products, including yoghurt and cheese, are all sour items.

Next is salt taste (*lavana*) and these items of food will be in the *dosha* category of *pitta*. As in sour foods, salty items will keep the *vata* under control but, on the other hand, care needs to be taken as too many salty items in our diet will tend to disorganise the *pitta dosha*. All types of salt will come under this heading, including both sea and rock salt.

Air and space is contained in the taste of bitter (*tikta*), so that items containing bitterness will increase the influence of the *dosha vata*, which is the predominant *dosha* of the three. As suggested by the category of air and space, the items of diet will by their very nature be of lightness. Such foods will tend to reduce weight in our bodies but, if taken to excess, can cause serious loss in weight and also weakness. In the bitter taste are included greens, lettuce and vegetables, including spinach, brussel sprouts, swiss chard, and the bitter herbs including sorrel, fenugreek, aubergines and rhubarb. The bitterness of many of these items will vary one from another, so that certain categories appear to us to be more bitter than others.

Next are the pungent (*katu*) or hot and really spicy foods. These foods have fire and air in them, and affect both *vata* and *pitta doshas* while, at the same time, subduing the effects of *kapha*. These can reduce the excessive building of fatty tissues but excess consumption of such pungent, hot or spicy foods can result in excessive thirst. Because of the build-up of excessive *doshas pitta* and *vata*, there can be a tendency to aches and pain. Under this category are peppers, chillies as well as ginger, parsley, dill and camomile, as also are many of the essential oils.

The last of the types of taste is that of astringent (*kashaya*). Substances which are astringent will be of the elements earth and air. They will be dry by their nature, or can cause dryness in the body. Honey is an astringent, although in its nature it is very sweet.

The Six Tastes and Their Effect on the Doshas

TASTE	AFFECTING THE *DOSHAS*	MAJOR EFFECT	FOOD
⑧ SWEET (earth and water)	+ *Kapha* − *Pitta* − *Vata*	Anabolic and can increase weight	Rice, sugar (unrefined) eggs, milk
✳ SOUR (earth and fire)	+ *Pitta* − *Vata* + *Kapha*	Good for the digestion (*agni*)	Tomatoes, citrus fruits ~~dso~~ cheese + yoghurt
✳ SALTY (water and fire)	+ *Pitta* − *Vata* + *Kapha*	Good for improving taste	Fish, salt
∅ BITTER (air and space)	− *Kapha* + *Vata* − *Pitta*	Can reduce weight	*Methi* (fenugreek) spices Leafy vegetables
✳ PUNGENT (air and fire)	+ *Vata* + *Pitta* − *Kapha*	Stimulates hunger	Pepper, chillies & ginger
∅ ASTRINGENT (air and earth)	+ *Vata* − *Kapha* − *Pitta*	Good for complexion, skin	Honey

✳ heat the body
∅ cool the body

56

6
The Food Chain

In the Ayurveda routine of proper eating an important habit to acquire is *samskaras* (repeated actions or tendencies). At a higher level, in terms of Ayurveda philosophy, eating is an act of daily sacrifice. This sacrifice is not to an altar fire, but to one's own internal fire. It is almost impossible to construct healthy and good tissues from food that is not good or is not healthy. However, the individual's point of reference – all the factors involved in the makeup of that person, the personality type and so on – has to be borne in mind.

In contrast with the position today, there was once much more home-grown fruit and vegetables in gardens and allotments. It was easier to obtain produce that had been grown locally and in many cases with little or no pesticides or chemical fertilisers.

Now we have to rely much more on others, on shops and supermarkets for our food needs. Commercial growers supply the produce for these retail outlets. For a variety of reasons we do not grow fruit and vegetables ourselves but this situation may slowly be altering, as more and more people begin to realise and appreciate the value of home or locally grown food. Interest is now being shown also in organic fruit and vegetables in this country.

As for the vitally important task of cooking food, we have to rely completely on the cook, be it ourselves or someone else, to serve us in the preparation and cooking of the food. The role of the cook is important in Ayurveda as it is in cooking everywhere.

All the world over a good cook can improve the taste and the qualities of almost any type and standard of food. The effect of food on us will in the end rely completely on the strength of our digestive capacity. In the first place all food enters the stomach in a so-called raw stage, after which it is then 'cooked' inside us. Until it is properly digested, it can be poisonous. Only after it has been properly 'cooked' by the system will food become pure and fit to be assimilated into the body, and the resultant nutrients later taken up to nourish the tissues.

Charaka said every action of food on the body is the result of potency or, in other words, its physical power, influence, and the energy it gives and projects upon the body system. The four main potencies or influences are whether food is heavy, light, hot or cold. In the case of food classified as hot or having a hot nature, this will give more fire to the body, while naturally cold-nature food will reduce heat. Generally, sour, salty and pungent foods are hot substances, while sweet, bitter and astringent sub-stances are cold.

There are three stages in which food goes through the human system during digestion and its later absorption into the body. Firstly, there is the raw material, the food in the stomach, controlled by the *kapha dosha*, and of which the main taste is the sweet one. Then, secondly, the actual digestion or 'cooking' stage in the small intestine under the control of *pitta dosha*. Here we have the yellow bile and the sour taste. The 'cooked' stage then comes next, with the pungent taste being the strongest, and which is under the control of the *vata dosha*.

In the important post-digestive effects, we have, firstly, the influence of the sweet *kapha dosha* on building up of the tissues. Next, the sour bile, which may reduce or burn away the tissues. Lastly, there is *vata* with its dry and moody nature, with the inherent tendency to cause a drying out of the tissues and the body.

Our choice of food is mainly influenced by taste and it is possible that what we are looking for is a taste or quality in the food that may be lacking in ourselves. No one food is suitable for everyone because of different times, climates and seasons, and the important constitution factors that we need to consider. We may want or like a certain taste, a certain food, but we need to be more widely informed.

Past habits, emotions and conditioned preferences will demand specific foods of a particular taste, but the problem with that is the body also wants and demands that taste. This is fine but only in so far as food with that taste contains food's other qualities, whether it is hard or soft, heavy or light, oily or dry, and whether its chemical content for the body to remain in balance is provided. It is better to know what you really *need* and make the selection accordingly, rather than to permit your mind to convince you that the things it likes will be good for you and for your body. Mistakes can be made, but having a general plan does help, taking into account the varying factors of the food's natural purity and quality, its preparation and cooking, the quantity, the time, the season, the climate, the general rules of eating and the rules relating to the eater.

Although the natural qualities of good food are important, a lot will also depend on food preparation. Again, there is *samskaras* – tendencies developed by repeated actions.

These tendencies or actions can be good or bad, but the aim is also to develop good *samskaras* of the cook in preparation of food. In cooking, the qualities of the food can be altered far more than we realise. For example, milk can be lightened when heated with the spice saffron. We know that rice or porridge will be made heavier when cooked with milk, instead of water. Honey should never be heated, as it is already a 'hot' food. The aim in Ayurveda is the prevention of possible problems or side-effects of food, by taking the proper action, the *samskara*. Lemon will often be served with fish to make fish less likely to aggravate *dosha pitta*. Turmeric is added to beans and lentils as there can be a tendency for these to affect the blood, although otherwise they are very good foods with lots of protein. Ginger, garlic and asafoetida will all help in preventing *vata* imbalance. The use of a *vaghar* preparation in Indian cooking is widespread, not only adding flavour to the food, but balancing the three *doshas*. Spices, condiments and herbs are much used in the Indian subcontinent, not only to assist balancing the *doshas* but also to help in the supply of minerals needed by the body. It is therefore good if we are able to use at least some of these spices, herbs and condiments in our cooking, in keeping with Ayurveda.

Charaka gave a number of fundamental rules on the nature of food and its eating:

1 Generally, eat food that has been cooked, as this will help to stimulate digestion.
2 Eat unctuous food, which stimulates the digestive fire, and food that is nourishing.
3 Eat food in proper combination and due measure. This should be done after full digestion of the previous meal. In other words, there should always be

the all-important gap between meals. This guidance is made because there must always be a free passage available for all substances.

4 Eat in pleasant surroundings, and in a quiet atmosphere whenever possible. This can either be alone or with friendly or affectionate people, so that the mind is relaxed and uplifted.

5 Do not eat hurriedly or too slowly. Think about the food you are eating.

6 Eat without talking or laughing, and with concentration and due consideration to your constitution, and as to what is good or bad for you, and the time you are eating it.

The statement that we are what we eat is fundamental to the system and philosophy of Ayurveda, the science of life. In Ayurveda it is rightly recognised that nothing could be simpler than realising the fact that the food we put into our mouths matters and that food in the longer term will have a profound influence on our bodies and upon our consciousness.

Food can be used as an addition or substitute for love, comfort and as an emotional substitute for something that may be lacking in us. An occasional reduction in food intake, or a complete fast, does help the body in the process of purification, with a resting of the digestive system, and can help in the renewing and heightening of the taste sensation. It can also help in developing a better overall approach to eating.

In India today many people undertake fasting, say for one day a week or month. It is part of a tradition there in what may be termed a more reverential approach to food. This attitude is also in line with the general philosophy of

Ayurveda. However, longer fasts are not considered good as uncontrolled complete fasts can cause degeneration of body tissues, and can also result in a serious loss of co-operation and cohesion between the body and mind.

Habit is a very pronounced feature of food and our eating procedures. We can aim to maintain health by developing good eating habits and by choosing a good and sensible diet. Charaka said that in general you should become addicted to unctuous food that includes all the six tastes. If you drift into eating most of your food of one taste, this can develop into a problem for you: your vitality and resistance will be low. The body will, in the short run, learn to cope with incorrect food and diet, and know that you will be eating a particular food on a regular basis. Some negative effects will still be experienced by us, but the body learns how to cope with these problems of incorrect diet, reorganising itself and creating a new metabolic balance, based on the food coming to the body and its need to take action.

The body will sweep the poisons into storage, where they can later cause chronic disease. Paradoxically, we ourselves will feel acute discomfort when these poisons are not entering the body system on a regular basis. In other words, there can be a withdrawal system in operation when we remove incorrect foods and attempt to put our diet to rights, similar to that experienced by those dealing with cases of alcohol, drug and tobacco addiction. Therefore Ayurveda says that we should try to reach the habit of feeding ourselves with good food, getting into the habit of actually being addicted to good food, and only letting in poisons occasionally or for medical use.

Charaka once said that sugar was a food that could be safely used on a regular basis but we see now that this wonderful commodity has become greatly over-used. Its negative qualities are now threatening to overtake its good qualities. Over-use, misuse and abuse of foods has become an increasing burden in recent years, so much so that sometimes people who are sensitive to certain foods have now become allergic to them. The habit of taking in unhealthy foods can be eliminated, but it is better to eliminate them on a gradual basis. It appears to be a factor in today's living that more and more people are becoming addicted to many more foods and substances.

7
Balancing of Foods

It is the act of balancing the diet that is most vital for maintaining a state of well-being. In food we have not only the ingredients but also the qualities of the *doshas* in the food, that is *vata, pitta* and *kapha*, which are found everywhere in nature. In dealing with balance we find out, firstly, to which type of constitution we belong, realising that everyone is slightly different. Some adjustment may then be needed in our choice of food and diet to get our balancing act together.

We obtain from Ayurveda information and guidance to foods and combinations of foods that are needed, taking into account the time, season, and individual circumstances, and the general tendency relating to the constitution type we come under. Having completed the questionnaire, most people find that no overwhelming type is presented, but that they will score under all the *doshas*, although one or more appearing to have some dominance over the others. It is this influence that has to be corrected through our choice of food.

Destroying or Subduing Doshas
There are foods that will subdue and in some cases destroy *dosha* elements in other foods, helping in the act of balancing the three elements. With practice you will be able to

sense the need to increase, reduce, subdue or neutralise the effect *doshas* are having on the system as a whole. This feeling will come as a kind of intuition, enabling you to act accordingly. As already indicated, there are a number of different factors relating to this essential balancing of the *doshas* in each individual, one of which is our constitution type and another, the climatic conditions – the parts played by the weather, time of year and the different seasons.

Subduing Vata
Firstly, there are foods that subdue or destroy the *dosha vata*. They include fresh ginger, ginger powder, fresh butter, salt, milk, yellow marrow, dates, sugar, carrots, wheat, yoghurt, black grapes, oranges, coconut, almonds, lemons, small aubergines, string beans, apple, asafoetida (*hing*), unripe fruit, green bananas, apple and oranges.

Generally *vata* people have some difficulty with the digesting of raw vegetables and salads. To achieve a balance and to avoid any problems, you should avoid cold foods, including cold or iced drinks; all these should be reduced or avoided altogether. The tastes that you should be considering in your food are those of salty, sour and sweet tastes. Foods that are required to achieve balance will be heavier foods that have an oil content in them, including a lot of hot dishes, especially nourishing stews, baked dishes and good hot, nourishing soups. Bear in mind that the *vata dosha* is made up of air and space or ether, for this aspect is significant and controls motion in our body. *Vata* really is the boss and does influence the other two *doshas* of *pitta* and *kapha*. Some *vata* types of constitution can have problems with digestion. Easily digested foods are therefore the order of the day; those which will help regulate *agni*, the digestive fire. *Vata* types are rather sensitive to pressure and tension, so that whenever possible, meals should be taken in as calm and relaxed surroundings and atmosphere as possible.

Subduing Pitta

Food which regulate *pitta* will include cucumber, unripe banana, wheat, milk, coconut, water, string beans and apples. Sour fruits and sour dairy products, such as yoghurt and cheese, should be reduced or avoided. The *pitta dosha* is hot so that people of this constitutional type need to eat cool and refreshing foods in the summer months. Food items that produce heat in the body should be brought under control or drastically subdued, including salt, oil, pungent seasoning and spices, especially during hot summer weather. In warmer times, *pitta* types will be able to keep the *pitta dosha* under control with green salads. Regularity of eating is the order of the day for *pitta* people, who should not miss meals because they are too busy or under stress.

Subduing Kapha

Food that will subdue or destroy *kapha* include unripe bananas, dates, carrots, buttermilk, honey, black pepper, mustard seed, lemon, salt butter beans, ginger powder, asafoetida (*hing*) and sweet melon. Generally speaking, *kapha* types have good appetites, and there is a possibility of eating too much (see page 18). Because of this, with many sweets and foods that are fatty, there can be a good chance of putting on weight over a prolonged period, so that *kapha* types need to include in their diet some foods that have the bitter and pungent tastes, including methi, lemon, ginger, pepper and some spices. There is a tendency to avoid these two tastes a lot, and this is a reason why many problems increase later in life. The *kapha dosha* can be increased by the heavier and oilier types of foods and also by cold foods.

To rectify and pacify the *kapha dosha*, everything that is of a light nature, dry and hot, will be good. This constitutional type should aim to eat low-fat and lightly cooked dishes, with plenty of raw vegetables and fresh fruit. As there can be a tendency for *kapha* types to be overweight, they will be able to skip meals occasionally without too much discomfort. The pungent, bitter and astringent tastes will have a balancing and good effect on the *dosha*.

Increasing or Producing Doshas
Here we have foods that are capable of increasing or producing the different elements of *vata, pitta* and *kapha* although, in many cases, a dominance of one *dosha* may not be very pronounced, so only a slight adjustment will need to be made.

Increasing or Producing Vata
Where *vata* needs to be increased or produced, the following foods can be included: spinach, honey, all kinds of beans, dry vegetables (salad type), cornflakes, lemon, parsley, salt, squash, tea. Dryness being a quality in *vata*, the tendency is that anything of a light nature, such as salad, raw vegetables and cold drinks, will intensify the *dosha vata*. Where an increase or balancing in *vata* is required, these foods should be taken and given full consideration.

Increasing or Producing Pitta
Producing-*pitta* foods include: butter beans, salt, water melon, sesame seeds, sprouted beans, dry vegetables and asafoetida (*hing*).

Increasing or Producing Kapha
Kapha producers include sugar, sesame seeds, milk,

oranges, string beans, dry vegetables, apples, cauliflower, spinach, turnips and tomatoes.

The listings of foods below come under the three *doshas* of *vata*, *pitta* and *kapha*. Some foods contain more than the one property and these are listed separately. There are a small number of foods that could be described as perfect, as they contain an almost equal amount all three *doshas*. One of these is milk but to contain the three properties, the milk must be very fresh indeed, obtained from the cow on the same day, and the present distribution system does not allow for milk in that condition to be available.

Vata Dosha Foods

Beans (all kinds)
Broccoli
Cabbage
Cornflakes
Honey
Lemon
Parsley
Salt
Spinach
Squash
Tea

Pitta Dosha Foods

Asafoetida (*hing*)
Butter beans
Celery
Chocolate
Coffee

Cucumber
Curds
Dry Vegetables
Melon
Mint
Onions
Parsnips
Peas
Peanuts
Pickles (sour and hot)
Potatoes
Pulses
Salt
Sesame seeds
Soya beans
Sugar (raw or unrefined)
Sunflower seeds
Tamarind
Vinegar
Walnuts
Wheat

Kapha Dosha Foods

Avocado
Cabbage
Cauliflower
Grapefruit
Green leaf vegetables
Honey
Kelp
Lettuce
Milk (bottled or cartoned)

Mushrooms
Oranges
Pears
Rice
Spinach
Sugar
Swiss chard
Tomatoes
Turnips

Foods Having Vata/Pitta Properties

Bananas
Sugar (refined)

Foods Having Vata/Kapha Properties

Apple
Beetroot
Carrots
Chestnuts
Corn
Cream cheese
Dates
Grapes
Oatmeal
Olives (ripe)

Foods Having Vata/Pitta/Kapha Properties

Cream (fresh)
Black pepper
Fish
Milk (fresh, whole)

Protein and Carbohydrates
Ayurveda recognises the vital importance of the nutritional content of food but emphasises that there is more to food than consideration of the proteins and carbohydrates – there are also natural qualities in all foodstuffs. This philosophy is found in the ancient writings and the traditions of India, which give specific details of these qualities, and which are essential in helping to maintain the state of wellness, well-being and health.

Qualities or properties in food noted in Ayurveda include the following:

1 *Quickly Digested Foods*
Ginger, carrot, rice, buttermilk, black pepper, lemon, small aubergines, dry ginger, turmeric, asafoetida, apple, puffed rice, white radish.

2 *Harder to Digest Foods*
Tamarind, cucumber, unripe banana, yellow marrow, dates, wheat, blackeye bean, water melon, yogurt, popcorn, spinach, potatoes, almonds, large aubergines, butter beans, string beans, sprouted beans, dry vegetables, milk, meat.

Included in the lists are perfectly good foods coming under the various *doshas*, but their nature is such that they are more easily digested than others, so that in the case of the harder to digest foods, more work is needed from the digestive system. Therefore more energy will be taken from us. In certain circumstances it will be advantageous to have foods that are easily taken into the system and easily digested. We know this to be the case when we are unwell and need to conserve our energy.

Hot and Cold

Another category under which foods are classified is as to whether they are hot or cold. This hotness or coldness does not relate to whether they have been cooked or remain uncooked, but refers to their essential nature, and their action in producing hotness or coldness within our body.

1 *Hot Foods*
Fresh ginger, ripe melon, sesame seeds, sesame oil, yogurt, white radish, mustard seeds, salt, aubergine, ginger powder, carrots, ripe melon.

2 *Cold Foods*
Bananas, dates, wheat, clarified butter (*ghee*), rice, spinach, split beans, black grapes, coconut, potatoes, puffed rice, butter, string beans, apple, rock salt, dry peas.

Increasing Digestive Power
Foods that increase the digestive power (*agni*) in the body, and also give the stomach help in good and correct assimilation of further food, are: ginger, buttermilk, sesame seeds, spinach, oranges, butter, lemon, black salt, ginger powder, asafoetida (*hing*), carrots, puffed rice, white radish, aubergine.

Added Strength
Strengthening and stimulating foods include ripe banana, dates, coconut, wheat, sesame seeds, milk, fresh butter, string beans, *ghee* (clarified butter), ginger, cabbage, basmati rice.

Easily Digested
There are some foods that are easily digested and, at the same time, will help in the binding of other foods in the

stomach: ginger, cucumber, carrots, yogurt, ginger powder and also the majority of fruits.

In general terms so-called heavy foods should form between one-third and one-half of your meal, then you can complete the meal and have your fill of foods that are light in nature. In any event, it is advisable to leave the last third of your stomach empty to allow the free movement of the *doshas*. In Ayurveda the amount of food we eat, the stomach capacity, is related to the strength of the digestive fire in the body, the *agni*, and not completely relating to the size of your stomach, or to the volume you have left to fill. Where there is a very good digestive fire, for example in the person having a strong *pitta* constitution, then such an individual can cope with almost any dietary indiscretion and get away with it. But not so *kapha* and *vata* types. In the chapter on constitution types (page 14) it was seen that we are a mixture of the three *doshas*, *vata*, *pitta* and *kapha*, and our task is to keep them in balance at all times of day and times of year.

8

Crimes Against Wisdom

Charaka said that everything in the world has only two conditions. One is the abnormal and other normal, and both are dependent upon a cause, and that nothing can happen in the absence of a cause. He also wrote at length on the theory and application of *karma,* or past actions, including the Hindu doctrine of reincarnation. He concluded that, although influences in previous lives and the present are important, rational therapy is only useless if the patient is medically incurable.

From the start, it is seen that the philosophy of Ayurveda is deep, that although there is a further, spiritual dimension to the subject, its main role is the question of health. In the Christian sphere, Jesus pointed out that sins, or one's *karma,* can be forgiven and redeemed.

Non-apparent causes of diseases still exist in Ayurveda, and this is because some conditions cannot be explained reasonably by reference to the imbalance of the *doshas* only, and so remain open to query. This leaves the reason for the disease deeper in the organism than at the level at which the *doshas* operate.

In Ayurveda the main types of disease are:

1 Congenital, as in the case of deformities.

2 Metabolic, giving rise to an imbalance of the *doshas*, caused by excessive or insufficient intake of food or incorrect food and other nutrients.
3 Traumatic, which is caused by shock; either physical or mental or both.
4 Temporal or seasonal. Because of, or during the changes in the seasons, failure to protect by way of adjusting intake of food and diet. Other forces include astrological influences, including the action of the sun and moon.
5 Spiritual or divine. Not following the guidance of the guru or teacher. It also includes dark forces, and epidemics.
6 Natural causes. These will include hunger, thirst, fatigue, decay and lack of sleep.
7 Genetic or hereditary.
8 Tendencies that may or may not be realised or be difficult to diagnose.

Other than the metabolic cause of disease where, due to incorrect, insufficient, or excessive intake of food, the *doshas* have been upset, Ayurveda says that the fundamental cause of all diseases, other than the causative factors relating to diet, are due to desire. As the master Vagbhata says, 'All diseases begin with *raga*', which in English equates with the words desire, passion and heat. Desire is called the first of all diseases because it results in imbalance to contentment and disrupts the mind, drawing it away from the balance that it requires for health and wellness.

The other point made by Vagbhata was that all who wish to protect themselves from harm, affecting the great organ heart, channels and *ojas*, should try to avoid anything afflicting the mind. All this reflects the emphasis given to calmness leading to coolness, and explains the importance of relaxation and meditation for the overall consciousness. In a deeper sense, Ayurveda leads the way towards a spiritual philosophy, which is expanded many times in Indian classical writings, including the *Vedas, Upanishads*, and especially in the *Gita*, the epic of Indian philosophy.

Importance is giving to the idea of developing a sense of being satisfied, and creating in people a corresponding feeling of calmness leading to coolness in the consciousness. The problems generated by dissatisfaction, mainly in the realm of selfishness and selfish desires, will encourage the heat of passion, and this will in turn create an abnormal heat, disturbing levels in the organism or body, becoming manifest in physical or mental fever. Ayurveda is very clear on this, in describing the result as an actual heat or fever.

By heating the body, mind and senses, this fever or fervour in Ayurveda diminishes wisdom, strength, glow, vitality, liveliness, keenness and enthusiasm, and leads to physical and mental exhaustion and delusion, which will have a detrimental effect on nutrition. We therefore require coolness of mind to maintain ourselves in a state of general health, a state of wellness. Fever and excess emotions are the enemy and will incinerate the system, which is definitely what we do not want. The combination of hot and dry, relating to fever, will have a reaction on the body's juices (water and earth) with the result of obstructing the channels and aggravating the three *doshas*. The cause of all disturbance of the *doshas* is heat imbalance; fever or heat is the only true disease.

The six tastes are in control of physical and mental digestion and under the control of our emotions, so that what is taste in our food and diet will translate into emotion on the mental plain. The Charaka treatise on the nature of disease is filled with accounts of the pathology of eight diseases caused mainly, whether directly or indirectly, by greed, malice and anger: haemorrhagic diseases and phantom tumours, fever, diabetes, other urinary disorders, skin diseases, insanity and convulsions.

A disease is therefore a living reality that has been created from our own mental and physical wastes, and which has taken on a life of its own through a combination of circumstances born of desire, seasonal differences, mental perversity, not only dietary problems and indiscretions. Some diseases will have physical presences, including those caused by bacteria or viruses.

Ayurveda goes into the depths of the question of our personalities, and says that many of us otherwise quite 'normal' people will have a number of sub-personalities, any one of which can surface at different times. All these sub-units are in touch with each other, and most of us will not suffer from the grave problems people with split or multiple personalities have to contend with. This means that most of us can cope pretty well as being 'normal' in society, although at the same time we cannot claim to enjoy a complete integration of consciousness and wholeness. This complete wholeness, which is quite rare, will be seen in a person who has developed in a totally spiritual way, or who can be, or has in the past, been reckoned a saint or seer, having passed over his or her nature to the will of God, the Divine nature, the Absolute Being or Force in the Universe.

Prajnaparadha in Sanskrit means 'crimes against wisdom', and is a word that reflects a great deal about the basic thinking behind the philosophy of Ayurveda. On an ordinary level it means going against good sense, judgement or common sense, such as getting very cold or wet, or going outside in certain adverse weather conditions. These are problems due to allurement and the idea of the ourselves, the microcosm, ignoring the inherent rhythm of the universe, the macrocosm, and attempting to rearrange the universe to suit ourselves.

A mistake against wisdom, or rather a crime against wisdom, also takes into account sins, which are volitional transgressions. The difference between a sin and *prajnaparadha* is that the former implies guilt, whereas *prajnaparadha* stands back in an impartial way, and views the self as being unwilling, or not having the ability to remain in, or come into harmony with, the cosmos or universe. The task therefore is to take on the responsibility of improving the situation for yourself and work out this improvement gradually. Guilt is no part of the philosophy in Ayurveda, as it can lead to a position of limiting yourself, rather than overcoming any problems, getting on with the job, and learning by listening to nature.

Prajnaparadha, this perversity of mind, is the final cause of every disease, and can affect speech, body and mind directly. It also works indirectly through improper contact of the sense organs with outside factors such as noise, rain, weather, listening to noises that frighten, or seeing things or sights that otherwise distract or disturb the body or mind or both. Again, problems arise in not paying proper attention to changes in diet, and in the style of living demanded by differences in weather and the seasons.

At a higher level, neither the senses, for example seeing and hearing, cause any pain or pleasure in themselves, rather in their contact with outside factors of noises and sights. We cannot blame macrocosm (nature and the universe) or microcosm (the living unit), but rather the fault lies in the relationship between these two fundamentals.

Not using the sense organs correctly and inattention to

the time and the seasons are secondary to *prajnaparadha*. The crime against common sense has been let in by desire, the rage or fever – it is this which will lead to the imbalancing of the *doshas*. It is therefore the *doshas* that cause the unbalancing and vitiate all the elements of the body, or the already created tissues making up the body (the stationary items); the food and mobile elements; and the digested nutrients that are ready and needed to nourish the tissues.

In the changing world of today, there are many wonderful and beautiful things to see, and in the field of human endeavour much progress has been made. The natural beauty of the world can be a never-ending source of joy to many. We can see on all sides problems to contend with, in the shape of strong causative factors that include: imbalanced diets, noise, pervasive pollutants, including those of a chemical or magnetic nature, artificial light, too much physical activity, side-effects of medical treatments, an over-dependence on machines, poor architecture and colours that do not harmonise. There is the problem of too many negative thoughts and the continual information that is now being given out by way of television, radio, newspapers, magazines and the internet. If we allow it to happen, this deluge can be a drain on our energies as we try to absorb everything. The result can lead to an aggravation of the three *doshas*.

As far as the *doshas* are concerned, they can be normal, increased or decreased in their strength. It would certainly appear that most people here in the UK and in Europe are suffering from increased *doshas* because we are attempting to take in more than we can properly digest, in terms of food and information, that is, both physically and mentally. The *doshas* do not upset each other; it is the outside factors coming in that do the upsetting and are the cause of any imbalance in them. The *doshas* themselves have mutual and natural immunity.

Where food and diet are not right, and you can quantify this in relation to the different factors and conditions that occur day by day, monthly, yearly, according to age, and to digestive power, then there can be problems, which in reality is *ama*.

9

The Cradle Land

Ayurveda has a rich heritage. It is a vast scientific system in its entirety and the Sanskrit language, in which it was originally written, is itself a treasure house. That ancient classical language of India is regarded in much the same way as Latin, the classical language of the Western world. However, Sanskrit has within its borders a vast array of ancient literature, including the foremost religious and philosophical works in India, the *Vedas*, of which Ayurveda, the science of life, is a small part. Among the early fathers of Ayurveda are the original practitioners of that science and art, Charaka, Sushruta and Vagbhata.

In a television programme some years ago, the late Sir Mortimer Wheeler gave a fascinating account of the important archaeological discoveries that he and his team had worked on at Harappa, Mohenjo Daro and Taxila, after the Second World War. The digs uncovered further evidence of the ancient cities apparently built on the ruins of their predecessors. The earlier ones were believed to go back in time to the period of Indian civilisation in the years 7000 BC–9,000 BC. Some of the gold ornaments found at Taxila and other sites were so well finished and highly polished that they might have come out of a Bond Street jeweller's shop window rather than from a prehistoric house of some 7,000 years ago.

The archaeologists found ancient street and dwelling houses equipped with bathrooms, floored in brick and with good drainage systems, as well as wonderful jewellery. All this led to the conclusion that there had been a relatively high degree of luxury and social condition of the people, which appeared at the time to be much in advance of what was then prevailing in Egypt. Many authorities now place India as being the cradle of the human race. The early historian Avinash Chandra Das states that men were already living in a high state of civilisation when the Arabian Sea stretched far and wide, covering a large part of what is now the Indian state of Rajasthan. There was also another ocean system covering the regions in the northern part of the Himalayas, of which only very small parts now remain.

Earlier this century the Indian writer, U P Krishnamacharya, in his *Essays on Ancient India* made many interesting observations. He describes the Persians in their sacred works, *Vendidad* and *Zend Avesta*, mentioning that their forefathers had migrated to Persia from their original home, Hepta Hendu, or India. In the case of the Egyptians, they believed that their ancestors lived originally in the sacred 'Land of Punt', on the shores of the great Eastern Sea from where they migrated and, aided by their gods, finally settled on the banks of the Nile.

Again, there is the case of the Greeks, who were perpetuating a tradition that their forefathers came by a northern route and settled in various places, including parts of Greece, such as Athens and Sparta. As for the Latians, they believed that they had migrated to Latium, an ancient province in Italy, from the Asiatic coast, before the fall of Troy, and that the historically famous Romans were only a sect among these Latians.

Then there are the Scandinavians, who held the distinct view that their progenitors were immigrants in Scandinavia, having endured much trial and danger from their far-off home in the East, and were led by their chief who was called Gotma.

There is the situation where the ancient Druids of Great Britain were remembering that they were merely settlers in this country, and wore a crescent mark to denote their descent from the lunar race while they were in their fatherland. Again, the famous Aztecs of Mexico said that their ancestors came from a far-off land on the shores of the great Eastern sea, and then settled in what is now known as Mexico. We see a situation whereby many, if not all, of the nations in the world appear to describe their ancestors as having originally come from some Original Home, and that is India.

As far as Indians are concerned, India has for ever been the home of her people. What is being said is that the very creation of organic life occurred in the Aryavarta, the land of the Aryan Origin, in the area of the north-west of India where the famous rivers, especially the great Indus river, still flows.

The ancient Sanskrit works give an accurate geographical description of the Cradle Land and mention all the important rivers and mountains. We are therefore forced to the irresistible conclusion that, as far as theological and legendary evidence is concerned, India must be the 'cradle' of the human race.

The civilisation of China is considered to be one of the most ancient in the world, according to many Western sources of knowledge and scholarship. Equally, other sources give that civilisation as an offshoot of ancient Indian civilisation. Professor Terrien de Lacouperie, in his book *Western Origin of the Early Chinese Civilisation*, believes that, some 2,500 years ago, the Indian Brahmins, Kshatriyas and Vashyas colonised parts of China and founded powerful kingdoms there. In any event, we know that the early Indian merchants were honoured by the Chinese courts and did much to increase the relations of Indians with those trans-Himalayan colonists, and founded great trading links there.

According to H B Sarda, the *Vedas*, one of the most authoritative as well as being the revered ancient work in Indian literature, invites mankind to go to foreign countries in steamers and airships. In the *Yajur Veda*, Adhyaya 6, Mantra 21, it says: 'Oh men, who are fit to do administrative work righteously, go to the seas in big and fast going steamers, and to the high heavens in airships built on scientific principles.'

In the Hindu genius it is hard to find any branch of science that was not covered by those ancient scholars, including art and architecture, steel manufacturing, the art of warfare both in war and peace, and painting and weaving. In their great epics, as set out in the *Ramayana* and the *Mahabharta*, the realm of philosophy is seen as being the most comprehensive covering all possible solutions to the mysteries of the nature of man and the universe. The same applies to the subject of mathematics, the ancient scholars being the inventors of the decimal system and the zero.

In this remarkable climate of achievement and learning, it was only natural for the ancient Hindus to gradually develop a system of medicine consistent with their many other scientific developments. Unlike some other sciences, it was seen to have grown from an inward desire, not from any foreign or outward pressures. Good health, a state of wellness, is a priority in any country. This flight from ailments and diseases is common everywhere and has gone on in every country in the world.

The effort to learn and to cure did not wait upon some earth-shattering event or discovery, and is therefore usually considered to be in the nature of a gradual progress with experiments in trials and learning. There is a tradition in India that Ayurveda is of divine origin, being revealed to Brahma at the time of the Creation. Be that as it may, medicine was dealt with on a large scale in the *Vedas*, in the form of hymns to various plants, potent in the cures of various diseases. Over a long period, say from at least 3,000 BC, India has therefore given to the world a great benefit in medicine, an essential branch of learning.

It would be expected that a science such as Ayurveda would have its views and theories on the important problems of the evolution of the cosmos. The Ayurveda theory of Evolution appears to be a combination of the Sankhya, Patanjala, Nyaya and Vaisheshika systems of Indian philosophy in their most scientific aspects. The early work by Dr Brajendranath Seal, *The Positive Sciences of the Ancient Hindus*, sets out the thoughts of the early Ayurveda writers on the important question of evolution.

The ancient writers on Ayurveda certainly had their conception of evolution and appeared to be more or less in agreement in general terms. Taking the manifested universe and in our case the immediate solar system, this can be traced to the unmanifested ground, which in Sanskrit is called *prakriti*, conceived and considered as formless, limitless, indestructible, undecaying, ungrounded and uncontrolled, without a beginning and without end. The unity of *prakriti* is a mere abstraction as it is in reality an indeterminate and infinite continuum of infinitesimal *reals*.

The *reals*, which are qualities, or *gunas*, are divided into:

1 *Sattva*, which manifests itself in a phenomenon and has a tendency towards manifestation. It is therefore an essence which serves as the medium for the reflection of intelligence.

2 *Rajas*. This is more easily understood, it being energy which is efficient in a phenomenon, with the tendency to do work and overcome resistance.

3 *Tamas*. This is mass, or inertia, which counteracts the tendency of *rajas* to do work, and also of *sattva*, in its task of conscious manifestation.

Sushruta described *prakriti*, the ultimate ground, in the following way: 'Progenitor of all creation, self-begotten, connotation of the three *reals, sattva, rajas* and *tamas*. Existing in eight forms; the sole cause or factor in the evolution of the universe.' It is also described as beginningless, endless, limitless, inconceivable, unknowable, formless, everlasting and indestructible, unexcelled and ubiquitous.

What we are saying about the three *gunas* is that they are the sole constituents of *prakriti*, the ultimate ground, and they are the ultimate factors of the universe. An important point is that, although the three *gunas* are conceived to be substantive entities, they are not in themselves self-subsistent or independent entities, but considered to be interdependent moments in every real or substantive existence. Energy itself is substantive in this sense as it does not possess inertia or gravity. The nature of energy is therefore ultimately kinetic.

These three qualities of *sattva, rajas* and *tamas* do enter into everything in close union with one another, as the essential constitutive factors. The *gunas* are continually moving, always uniting, separating and again uniting. Everything in the world is the result of their rearrangement and their combination. They are in varying quantities in relation to their essence, energy and mass, with their various groupings, mutual interaction and interdependence. But throughout, although this close co-operation is going on continually in the world of effects, these different tendencies never unite, they never coalesce to form any new quality. Therefore the element is of *rajas* and *rajas* alone, and similarly *tamas* within its essential nature is in all matter giving resistance and stability and, lastly, *sattva* is given to all conscious manifestation.

Another important point is that of the natural interaction between the three *reals*. For example, so that there may be evolution with the transformation of energy, there must occur some sort of disturbance of equilibrium, and a preponderance of either *sattva, rajas* or *tamas*. The particular quality that happens to take the upper hand in any phenomenon will become manifest in that phenomenon, and the other two qualities will become latent, although their presence is known or inferred by their effect. Take, for example a moving object. It this case the *rajas*, the energy is predominant and to the fore (kinetic), while on the other hand the mass or resistance it offers is being overcome.

It is said that the starting point in the cosmic history is a condition of equilibrium, consisting of a uniform diffusion of the qualities or the *reals*. The tendencies to manifestation and work are exactly counterbalanced by the resistance of mass or inertia, and in that situation the process of cosmic evolution is under arrest. The process of evolution begins with the disturbance of the original equilibrium. The transcendental, or non-mechanical, influence of the *Purusha*, the Absolute, puts an end to this arrest, and initiates the process of creation. The qualities *sattva, rajas* and *tamas* possess a natural attraction for particulars of their own class, and

when the Absolute comes into play, it ends or breaks up this
uniform diffusion, and then leads to unequalness, and on
to the relative preponderance of one or more of the three
reals over the others. It then leads to a position of formative
combination among the *reals* and to productive activity. In
forming wholes, or systems, there must be an unequal
aggregation, which will overthrow the original equilibrium.

Sushruta mentions twenty-four fundamental principles
in the history of evolution. In addition, he says, there are
the same number of forms of *prakriti*, the limitless ultimate
ground. The individual soul descends under certain
concomitant conditions. Again Sushruta's conception and
idea of the individual soul is:

> The science of medicine does not lay down that the self-
> conscious selves are all-pervading, but on the contrary,
> it asserts that they are real and eternal and are born in
> the planes of divine, human, or animal existence
> according to their good or evil deeds in life. The existence
> of these self-conscious entities can be ascertained in as
> much as they are extremely subtle in their essence. The
> self-conscious self is possessed of infinite consciousness,
> is real and eternally subject to the process of being
> evolved out into a finite organic individual through
> the dynamics of the combined sperm and ovum.*

The master's statements on physiology are in the strictest
sense molecular and his statements on Ayurveda, the science
of life, an attempt to explain consciousness from the mate-
rialistic point of view. The intellect is also material. He says

*Reference work of Dr Brajendranath Seal on Sushruta. See in bibliog-
raphy his book *The Positive Sciences of the Ancient Hindus,* Motilal
Banarisdas, Delhi, reprint 1958.

that the soul has an independent existence, and that where there is life there is a soul, and it is not everywhere the same. The soul takes on board the sorrow, disease and death in its union with the body.

When considering the true nature and significance of the *tridosha* principle and its fundamental importance and value in Ayurveda, it is essential not to confuse it with a simplistic idea that it is wind, bile and phlegm. If only it were as simple and straightforward as that, but we know that the body functions are far more complicated.

Ayurveda contains several primary principles controlling the entire functions of the human body, on one side, the bio-motor force, or metabolic activity, and the preservation principle of the body or the immune system. On the other side, it gives the qualities of the three *gunas* which are fundamental and in control of all that is contained in the universe.

10
Through the Ages

Ayurvedic thoughts and methods have always made a deep impression on the people of the Indian subcontinent, and almost every home in the country is aware of the treatments available for common ailments. It is perhaps fair to say that there is no other country in the world, with the exception of the Chinese, where so-called folk medicine is so closely allied to official medicine. This is because Ayurveda has such a long history and is rooted in the people of India.

There, the selling of indigenous medicines totals over one and a half times that of modern remedies, and is a reflection of how much the Indian population rely on the traditional systems.

In a broader perspective, Ayurveda's ranking in the world league is not high, but its position in the Indian subcontinent is assured, notwithstanding the advance of modern medicine. Ayurveda suffered a setback with the introduction of Western-style medicine in India at the beginning of the nineteenth century. Up to that time the basis of all medicine in India was traditional, in other words, a combined practice of folk medicine and Ayurveda.

Ayurveda suffered during the period when modern medicine was evolving, because of the latter's method of subjecting all assumptions to experimental verification, testing and statistical research, after Cartesian scientific materialism was introduced into all fields of human endeavour and activity. Traditional medicine consists of real results and experiences, innumerable observations and many formulae, all of which reflect a wonderful mixture of inspiration, intuition and facts.

Modern medicine can also be said to have evolved from traditional methods over a long period of time. It is interesting to see in a World Health Organisation publication, John Canary remarked that the very earliest foundations of modern medicine, 'appears to include detailed description of medical conditions including diabetics, found in Vedic hymn'.*

At least one important feature of modern medicine, which distinguishes it from Ayurveda is the method of rigorously breaking down complex phenomena into their component parts and dealing with those parts singly and often in isolation. In other words, this approach is all the time looking for a single cause, and in ratifying this problem, will then be looking for the active principle to solve this problem from a therapeutic viewpoint. Modern medicine has developed this reductionist approach, instead of treating the patient as a complete human being. To be completely fair, today's doctor is indeed trained not to take anything for granted and to query or reject any observations that are not validated by modern scientific methods.

When looking at Ayurveda and present medical thought, it is striking to find that Ayurveda is in fact an extremely precise science, involved in many complicated exercises in

---

*'In Traditional Medicine and Health Care Coverage'. Editors Robert H. Bannerman, John Burton, Ch'en Wen Cheih, World Health Organisation, Geneva, 1983.

logic. This approach offers a system which presses the need for the promotion and preservation of health, to enable people to reach and maintain the highest possible standards in their well-being.

Original Ayurveda was written in Sanskrit but when Sanskrit was relegated to the status of a classical language many centuries ago, as was the case of Latin in the UK, Ayurveda became less familiar. In India a number of other reasons can be found for the lowering of Ayurveda's part in the general foundation of medical practice.

India has always remained a Hindu land, but with the Muslim conquest came the Unani system of medicine, although this was later to be much influenced by Ayurvedic practices. When British rule came to India, it prevented both the Ayurveda and the Unani systems continuing on their previous paths.

Although allopathy was introduced by the British, even this was based on the broader Ayurveda principles and philosophy. During the earlier part of the twentieth century, when the Indian people began their struggle for independence, headed by Mahatma Gandhi, because of the strong nationalistic views then held, many things British were rejected, including allopathy.

Allopathic medicines often give the opportunity and impression of offering so-called rapid cures, the medicines themselves being essentially symptomatic. The pharmaceutical industry has developed to allow medicines to be more palatable and easier to take and distribute. What is sad to recall is that often, along with the fuller introduction of Western-style medicines and with the changing lifestyle for people in India, these factors made it difficult for later generations of Indians to practise or accept Ayurveda.

There have been a number of reasons for the overshadowing of Ayurveda by modern medicines. The over-riding attitude appears to have been an endeavour to find out 'the how' and 'the why' in the cases of any observation that is not validated experimentally. However, the main object of this analysis is biological as in physio-chemical sciences, thereby to determine and isolate the conditions which bring about the occurrence of each of these phenomenon. In many cases, experience has shown that where we cannot arrive at a position beyond 'the how' the question 'why' is out of reach of our experimental science.

But in the last few years, more and more medical journals have included articles on so-called holistic medicine. Any uncritical rejection of science will not further or serve the cause of that science, neither will its uncritical acceptance. Such writing off of any question of reality outside of existing methods is really a poor denial of such a reality. It is hoped, therefore, that both the allopathic doctor and the Ayurvedic practitioner will be able to develop a genuine interest in each other's medical systems, which interest can then lead to some sort of combined research activities leading on to a much more integrated medical system here in this country. Perhaps we will them be heading forward to the World Health Organisation's plea of health for all originally by the year 2000, not withstanding the spending on the National Health Service in this country of over fifty billion pounds each year.

The origins of Ayurveda go back a long time; some Indian scholars put the period at around 5,000 BC. On the later exponents of Ayurveda, Charaka and Sushruta, we have a great deal more information. It was Sushruta, in the fifth to fourth century BC who wrote the first widely accepted standard textbook of Ayurveda, the *Sushruta Samhita*, which was in the form of a palm-leaf manuscript. In the second century, there was a revised *Sushruta Samhita*, Nagarjuna. Meanwhile, Charaka revised the textbook as *Agnivesha Samhita* in the first century.

These early writings dealt with the different aspects of Ayurveda, and included instructions relating to the preservation of health, cure of diseases, maintenance of life, and aimed for a state of happiness and well-being. The organisation of the material in Ayurveda early textbooks is strikingly similar to those on modern medicine.

Some milestones in the development of Ayurveda during the last two thousands years are:

AD 100	Revision of *Agnivesha Samhita*: Charaka
AD 200	Revision of *Sushruta Samhita*: Nagarjuna
AD 400	Translation of Ayurveda texts into Chinese
AD 800	Ayurveda translated into Persian and Arabic
1200	Commentary on the *Sushruta Samhita*: Dalhan
1300	A *Materia Medica* compiled, called *Dhanvantari Nighantu*. The beginning of the inclusion of mercury in therapeutics
1700	*Ayurveda Prakasha:* Madhava Upadhyaya. Compendia written by the author, giving a combination of the literature of the ancient, with a relatively recent period
1800–30	The first Ayurveda dictionary in Sanskrit, *Vaidyakashabdasindhu*: Umeshachandra Gupta
1860–70	Beginnings of the manufacture of Ayurveda drugs in India
1870–1900	Great efforts made to translate and disseminate Ayurveda into various regional languages, including Bengali, Marathi and

Gujarti. A large number of societies formed for the propagation of Ayurveda, and the foundation of the Ayurveda Society of India. The monthly journal, *Bhishag Vilasa* devoted to Ayurveda began.

Throughout the twentieth century a large number of researchers carried out valuable work in the field of Ayurveda; among them were: Major B D Basu, botanist, and Colonel K K Kirtikar, biologist. These two provided important studies of Indian medicinal plants, and this information was published in *Indian Medical Plants* in 1918. A revision was made by L M Basu, with the help of eminent scholars E Blatter, J F Cains and K S Mhaskar and this work resulted in four volumes that included 1,033 plants, with a photograph of each plant. This work of Kirtikar and Basu is now available in a set of four volumes of text (2,991 pages) and another four volumes containing 1,053 pages and 1,033 plates with line drawings, giving eight volumes in all. Later, Colonel Sir Ramnath Chopra gave special attention to investigating how indigenous drugs could be used as substitutes for those in the British pharmacopoeia. The results of his experiments, which laid the foundation of verification of ancient thoughts and practices, appeared in *Indigenous Drugs of India* in 1931. There have been many other research workers throughout India during the whole of the century.

Ayurveda suffered a setback in the first decades of the twentieth century, when it was overshadowed by the success of Western medicine. One of the problems was that Ayurveda did not offer rapid and effective therapies for the serious killer diseases, such as bubonic plague, smallpox and the many other bacterial infections that had been taking such a toll in the Indian subcontinent. To summarise, the position appears to have been brought about by the collective efforts of foreign rule and by the serious decline in the use of Sanskrit in which a large part of the texts on Ayurveda had been written. There was also a shortage of good printed teaching materials and a lack of good objective teaching methods in Ayurveda. All this led to a ready acceptance of allopathic medicine, especially in the urban population of India, where many middle-class and professional people are trained in Western medicine.

Ayurveda lost its drive, but it certainly never disappeared from the country, and in the rural areas it continued to play an important part in the health care of the people of India. It many ways Ayurveda medicine became intertwined with the local folk medicine. In any event, modern medicine is not presently available to a large part of the population, particularly in India's 550,000 villages, so that there is reliance on Ayurveda and herbal therapy.

Throughout the world, the last ten years or so have seen a dramatic increase of interest in all kinds of alternative systems of medicine, especially so in Ayurveda.

It is possible that the allopathic doctor in India would not turn to Ayurveda for the treatment of acute infections, but would be very tempted to try out therapies for chronic recurrent diseases, metabolic disorders and degenerative diseases, where modern medicine has less to offer.

As a result of interest in the use of medicinal plants in India and in other countries, there are now over 500 important periodicals published worldwide on the subject. This can in the long run only be good for the advance of Ayurveda and traditional medical systems. *Wealth of India* is one of the remarkable books to be published, a 20-volume encyclopaedia giving details of Indian raw materials and industrial products, and brought out by India's Council for Scientific and Industrial Research (CSIR, New Delhi, 1967).* In this series are included detailed articles on over 5,000 Indian plant species, of which over 2,000 are credited with possessing medicinal properties.

The number of medicinal plants used in the international market is now significant. In the UK market alone, there are over 3,000 herbal products covering at least 400 different kinds of herbs. Herbal preparations are even more popular in Europe, especially in Poland. This position is not at all surprising when it is considered that many Continental countries are in an advanced state of 'greenness'; in what has been described as having a 'green sweep'. What is important for Ayurveda is that it must be understood in terms of contemporary medicine, modified where it is found necessary to do so, and then practised according to its profound and ancient principles in their totality. It will then be in a position to be increasingly recognised as a major system of medicine.

*Reference Indian National Scientific Documentation Centre (INSDOC) 14, Satsang marg, New Delhi 110 067, which offers document copy supply and bibliographical services.

11

The Masters

Charaka, one of the early writers on Ayurveda, in the first century, said that the life of all living beings is food, and further that all the world is seeking food, and always has been. He wrote that all good and desirous things relate to and are established in food, especially good food, and these attributes to food include: complexion, clarity, a good voice, a long life, understanding, happiness, satisfaction, growth, strength and intelligence. He pointed out that all that is beneficial to the wider world happiness and also helping one to actions that can lead to spiritual salvation – all these things have their relationship and are established in food.

Charaka went on to say that it is evident that we treat a disease-ridden man or woman with disease-removing measures, and the depleted man or woman with impletion, nourishing the emaciated and the feeble, and starving the corpulent and the fatty. We treated the man afflicted by heat with cooling measures, and with hot things the person who is afflicted by cold. We replenish body elements that have suffered decrease, and deplenish those that have undergone increase. By treating disorders properly with measures which are antagonistic to their causative factors, this will restore the patient to normal.

In Ayurveda we may not obtain a perfect result every time, but the general idea and philosophy behind it is the daily offering of food to the human body and, in the highest reaches of this philosophy, offering food is a daily sacrifice to one's internal fire.

The three great Ayurveda master physicians of ancient times, Charaka, Vagbhata and Sushruta, laid the foundation stones of Ayurveda, the science of life:

Charaka
Disease is the disequilibrium of the *dhatus*. Disease is the disequilibrium of the *doshas*.

Vagbhata A.H. Su. 11:45
These very *doshas* which result in the growth of the body when they are in equilibrium, result in its destruction when in disequilibrium. For this reason, they are to be preserved by the beneficial conduct alone, for growth rather than for destruction.

Sushruta Su. 21:8
Just as the moon, the sun and the wind sustain the world by their acts of giving, taking and distorting, so do *vata*, *pitta* and *kapha* sustain the body.

Vagbhata A.H. Su. 1.6
In brief, *vata*, *pitta* and *kapha* are the three *doshas*. *Vata*, *pitta* and *kapha* alone are the causes (basis of) the formation of the body.

Sushruta Su. 21:3
By them alone when acting ('not dead' – functioning) the body is sustained.

Sushruta Su. 21.5
Kapha is composed of *apa* (water) and *prithvi* (earth).
The etymology of the word *kapha* is: *ka* means 'water'
and *pha* is the verb, *phalati*, which means 'derived from'.
Therefore we have *kapha*, that which is derived from
water.

Sushruta Sa. 15:45
The person who has *doshas, agni, dhatus* and *mala* in
equilibrium and who has sound soul, senses, and
mind is declared to be healthy.

Charaka Su. 30:26
The objective of this (science of Ayurveda) is the
preservation in health of the healthy and pacification
(the subsidence of the disease of the ailing).

Vagbhata A.11 Su. 11:1
Dosha, dhatu and *mala* form the foundational units of
the body.

Charaka Su. 9.4
The equilibrium of *dhatu* (tissues) is said to be normal
health.

Vagbhata A.H. Su. 1:20
The equilibrium of *dosha* is declared to be freedom
from disease.

Vagbhata A.11 Su. 11:2
Pitta is responsible for digestion, heat, vision, hunger,
thirst, taste, intelligence, courage, and soft supple body.

Sushruta Su. 14:12
Rasa (fluids) form the body therefore *rasa* should be
preserved with great efforts.

Vagbhata A.H. Su. 8:31–2
Excessive food diet is not the only cause of *ama*. Food which is hated, not served properly, burnt (overcooked) heavy, dry, cold, unclean, taken with excess water, is not digested. Also food that is consumed by a person tormented in grief, anger, hunger (this is not digested).

Charaka Su. 1:55
The body and that which is called the mind are both considered to be substratums (abodes) of diseases, likewise of well-being, and their concordance is the cause of well-being.

Vagbhata A.H. 11:35
Rasa vitiates *dosha*, *dosha* vitiates *dhatu* (tissue) and both vitiate *mala*.

Vagbhata A.H. Su. 12:32
Dosha is generally the cause for all the diseases.

Sushruta Su. 24:10
Vitiated *doshas* circulate in the body and the disease occurs in those tissues where they are obstructed due to their own abnormality.

Charaka Su. 9:6
Through knowledge of the science, keen observation and practice in various spheres (wide practical experience), skill and integrity are four qualities of the physician.

Vagbhata A.H. Su. 1:29
Attendants (nurses or assistants) should be devoted, clean, skilful and intelligent.

Charaka Su. 1:125
A drug whose name and form and properties are not known, and also when known, if improperly used, can produce disaster.

Charaka Su. 9:1–3
All substances are composed of the five basic elements. Therefore there is no substance in this world which cannot act as medicine.

Charaka Su. 26:52
One should not advise about the drug by advising about its *rasa* (taste) only (a drug does not act through *rasa* alone) because even when *rasa* (of drugs) is similar, actions of drugs may differ.

Charaka Vi. 1:13
A physician should have perfect knowledge of the causative factors, prodromal symptoms, evolution, differential diagnosis and severity of the disease. After studying this he should apply his mind (concentrate on) the specifications of the patient, such as *doshas*, region, build, diet, tolerance, *prakriti* (constitution) and age. The treatment depends on the knowledge of *dosha*, etc.

Charaka Vi. 1:19–20
Therefore the patient must be examined (from the point of view) of constitution, pathological condition, tone of the system, compactness, proportion, homologation, psychological factors, capacity for food, exercise, age, especially with a view to ascertaining the degree of his or her (the patient's) strength.

12
Vinoba Bhave on Food

Vinoba Bhave, the Indian social reformer (1895–1982), read his first book on Ayurveda in 1923, while he was in gaol at the time of the Flag Satyagraha, part of the non-co-operative movement against the civil authorities. A doctor in Ayurveda, who was a prisoner at the same time, helped Vinoba read the classic book by Vagbhata, written in Sanskrit. Later, Vinoba read the treatise by Charaka, the most meticulous observations made in those ancient times, written in a series of short sentences.

Vinoba once said that we do not often consider the kinds of food that will make the mind *sattvik*, that is, bright and clear. So the question remained, how can we aid the mind, keeping it pure, and the intellect clear? We are sometimes thinking about how to increase or maintain the weight of the body. The problem with weight is that it poses an additional strain on the heart, and this weight has always to be carried with us. The body is a tool and needs fuel enough to enable it to function properly but, at the same time, it does not need too much food. Over-feeding is a danger here and unnecessary, as the body can have difficulty in coping with this extra fuel.

In his book *Talks on the Gita*, written in 1932, Vinoba Bhave stated that to obtain true service to oneself and to society as a whole, purity in food should be realised as being necessary. As the food is, so is the mind or, in other words, Vinoba was saying that we are what we eat. In practice this statement may appear simplistic, but the subject does involve other considerations as well.

Vinoba had given his talks on the *Gita* while serving a further prison sentence in Nagpur gaol, where he had been imprisoned by the British Raj after supporting Mahatma Gandhi's non-co-operation movement, leading up to Indian Independence.

In addition to purity in food Vinoba went on to say that what mattered as well was to take into account the quantity of food taken, and that this was an important aspect of diet. The body mechanism will take care of most foods thrown at it, but it does not like over-supply, and will eventually kick against such misuse.

What we eat has a reaction. Why do we eat So that we can continue to live, and to give service to ourselves, our family and to the whole community. In India, food and cooking are also a form of sacrifice (*yajna*), and are looked upon as a kind of offering (*bhavana*). According to Vinoba, cooking requires both knowledge and love. In fact, three things are required in cooking – knowledge, love and the actual labour involved. All the activities of life will stand on these three aspects. These three factors are almost always present in the act of a mother's cooking, and that is why her cooking is always considered particularly tasty.

The cultures of the West and the East have long influenced each other, and this was the position even when Vinoba was writing about purity in food. He said that where absolute faith is shaken there need be no real harm done. Vinoba saw that what was good would remain, and the bad or unsuitable would be destroyed. But he also went on to say that blind unbelief should not be replaced by blind belief. Belief and unbelief, or misbelief – both of these can be blind as well.

Purity of food keeps the mind pure, and in this way the body will gain strength. Vinoba believed that the food we eat should be regulated, and in this not only is it important as to what food we have but also how much we eat. He said that, in his view, the question of how much food we take in is the more important question.

The position of the purity of food has not been improved in India today, with the opening up of the economy and the general increase in living standards. But great care has still to be taken on the question of purity in food. In Western Europe, and especially in the UK, there have been positive signs that the progress of vegetarianism has proceeded well. But in India the reverse may well be the case, with the increase and opening up of commercial outlets, and in the food retail organisations.

13

Revelations and Half-revelations

On nutrition and food-related subjects this country abounds with media stories and half-stories, of revelations and half-revelations about nutrition, food and food-associated subjects.

Fed on this diet of half-cooked information and half-ripe knowledge or no real knowledge at all, we attach ourselves wholly, sometimes partially, but always with feeling. If we feel so disposed we reject some or all of this information – including some or all contained in this book – and perhaps only believe such scraps of information, as either errors or containing some semblance of truth, that we can relate to.

The danger is that some of this misinformation may come to rest on us for some time, and in its wake a lot of damage may be caused. We ourselves are sometimes guilty of passing on non-proven information and titbits of intelligence to others, insisting that all is well.

The subjects of food production and farming, food distribution and marketing, taxation and duties and, above all, the availability of food, have caused economic, political problems and even wars in the past. It is little wonder that food manufacturers and processors have been viewed with suspicion during the past decades and the problem does not appear to be getting any better.

Many people regard some food as being harmful to them, and with due cause. The media can be a source of guidance, but at the same time can have an appetite for conflict and sensation. Many commentators and critics are often divided among themselves on the subject of presenting unscientific conclusions and results. All this information underlines the fact that the state of knowledge and thought about nutrition and purity in food is simply inadequate. On the one hand, there are vested interests, many of which are well intentioned, but the true positions can easily be obscured. The consumer is then faced with a bewildering number of choices.

Sometimes research into dietary effects and nutrition is completed by one country and then applied to another country, or to a section of its population. In some countries the amount of funding given over to research is large and in others limited and inadequate. The media will take up a story, and often find no research has been carried out either by the government departments or research bodies in that country.

The subject of nutrition as a serious life science and subject is important and not in question. The people engaged in this area, and the associated legislative bodies controlling and advising on food, have a considerable responsibility. Can we really be sure that the large multiples and supermarkets are friends of the consumer on the question of nutrition and the purity in food? What is self-evident, however, is the increasing amount of processed, ready-made foods, convenience food, fancy packaging and the ever-increasing amount of own-label brands on the shelves.

There appears to have been a shift in pressure and power

away from the growers, manufacturers and processors to the large multiples and supermarkets in their attempt to portray themselves as friends of the consumer. But in many instances what the consumer demands is cheaper food, and the supermarkets attempt to respond to this call. However, this should not be the sole criterion to food, this continuing demand for cheapness. Such an attitude in isolation could pose a serious and long-term danger and damage to the health of people.

The importance of purity in food and nutrition is a matter of education, starting in the primary schools or even earlier, and continuing on up through secondary schools, colleges and universities. This knowledge will later be used by local authorities and adult educational departments. The information available must be accurate and based on scientific research.

Where the food industry wishes to obtain and regain its credibility, steps need to be taken to fund independent nutritional research in our universities, which must be truly independent.

Research and development cost money; the large multiples and food giants have large resources but this research and education will surely pay off, and be beneficial both to the food industry and to the public.

The media will continue to play an important role in the future, as the public wish to hear and to see space given to informative and accurately researched articles, not limited to providing food scares and other information of an emotional nature.

One of the greatest problems facing the United Kingdom today is the huge cost to the state of the National Health Service. It is fair to suggest that even a modest increase in funding nutritional research by the government of the day can result in better health for people and with the resultant savings in the National Health Service. In the end we need the facts, knowledge, and thought rather than a continual trading of opinions.

14

Food as Medicine

Proper diet by its very nature will give nourishment to all the body, giving a good complexion, and heightening the senses. Failure to provide such a diet will discourage good health and, over a longer term, provoke disease. In Ayurveda it is said that a doctor who does not have the knowledge and the basic principles of dietetics cannot cure disease.

In the composition of food, people need two main categories. Firstly, there are the organic substances, which will yield energy by their oxidation and, secondly, inorganic substances, which are essential for the human body, and include salts and vitamins. Organic substances comprise:

1 Proteins essential to the generation and regeneration of bioplasm, the building material of the human body.
2 The saccharides, starches and sugars which we know as carbohydrates.
3 The fats.
4 The albuminoids.

The inorganic substances, which do not give energy in their oxidation, are:

1 Salts and vitamins, necessary for the nutrition of the body, and its bioplasm.
2 Extractives, which stimulate the gastro-mucous membrane and are needed for the nervous system in a general way.
3 Water, sometimes not given its proper place in the order of keeping the body systems in good order, but is essential to the bioplasm and for the circulation of the body fluids.
4 Roughage, fibre or ballast.

In the organic category of food, the first three parts, that is, the proteins, saccharides (carbohydrates) and fats, are structures of some complexity. They are substances charged with energy and, by their oxidation, converted or discharged into the various forms of heat, work and nervous energy.

The albuminoids are similar to protein but with the difference that, although they give energy by their oxidation, they do not build into bioplasm. In other words, they need replacement daily.

As far as the saccharides and fats are concerned, these can be dispensed with temporarily, for the reason that they can be obtained from proteins. The most important of all the substances are the proteins, salts, vitamins and water, all of which are essential to life.

Salts and vitamins by themselves do not provide energy but are important in providing nutrition for body building and maintenance of the bioplasm. Extractives mainly consist of broken-down proteins, and their tendency is to stimulate gastric digestion.

Water is a necessary part, making up all living tissues and consisting of around two-thirds of the entire body weight. It is also important for the circulation of food and waste products, and as a constituent of the secretion and excretion functions of the body. It also provides for losses in the evaporation from the skin and the respiratory tract. By this means, excessive heating of the body is prevented. Material which is unabsorbable, the bulk or ballast, is nevertheless essential to stimulate peristalsis, that is, good movement of the bowels.

Ayurveda can be categorised in another way, in order to account for all organic matter in the human body. All organic matter can be contained in the following five classifications:

1 *Mineral and nitrogenous compounds.* These include the following characteristics, either singularly or in combination: grossness; density; a high specific gravity; to be non-pungent, inert or rough; sharp-edged crystals, depending upon their axes; heavy, hard, odoriforous, slightly astringent and sweetish. Organic mineral bodies and protein can produce physical vigour (protein), hardness of bone structure (mineral) and muscular tissue growth (protein).

2 *Aquatic and water-bound substances.* These are ones that include the following characteristics: cool, moistening, soft, liquid, dense, smooth, acid or saline, sweetish, refreshing, moistening and adhesive.

3 *Hydrocarbons.* These substances contain the nature of being calorific, penetrative, fine textured, light, transparent, slightly acid and saline, pungent. They can cause combustion (oxidation and digestion), clearage (of food particles in the alimentary tube), heat radiation and bright complexion.

4 *Carbohydrates.* These substances can be described as

fine, desiccant, rough, crystalline, tactile, and can cause corpulence, muscular agility and relaxation.

5 *Ethers*. A substance that can be described as tenuous, rarefied, non-resistant (where a body passes through it). As a gaseous substance, it has neither size nor shape, and will diffuse itself into the surrounding area or into the atmosphere if it is not confined in a closed container. Transparent, made of diffused particles and tasteless.

For general guidance and reference purposes, the following foods and liquids can be used or not allowed in a diet for specific diseases, cases of ill health and where the three *doshas* have become disturbed and are out of balance in some way. Although these details are among the guidelines that the Ayurveda practitioner will refer to, other factors such as the sex, age, economic circumstance, lifestyle, constitution of the patient, must always be borne in mind.

Where you have an illness or medical condition, as opposed to following an incorrect diet, contact a registered medical practitioner or suitable therapist.

Acidity
Allowed: purgatives, water, sugar, wheat, bread, green vegetables, milk, butter, honey.
Not allowed: sour and salty foods, oils.

Anaemia and Jaundice
Allowed: rice, wheat, bread, butter, milk, sugar, honey, fruits, cream, water, cocoa, coffee.
Not allowed: cane sugar. Foods that are sour, pungent and salty. No dieting or fasting.

Biliousness
Allowed: milk, sugar, grapes. Fruits that are acid.
Green vegetables.
Not allowed: sour or oily foods.

Bronchitis and Chest Problems
Allowed: wheat, bread, butter, green vegetables, garlic,
grapes, hot water, currants, rice.
Not allowed: out in strong winds. Food that is too
heavy or too solid, any oily foods. Cold water.

Constipation
Allowed: fresh vegetables, bread, onions, cabbage,
apples, oranges, grapes.
Not allowed: potatoes, rice, milk, nuts, peas.

Diarrhoea and Dysentery
Allowed: fasting, rice, milk, butter, oranges, tea,
coffee.
Not allowed: any solid foods, potatoes, bread, green
vegetables. Exercise. Smoking.

Dyspepsia
Allowed: rice, fruits, green vegetables, salt, pungent
and sour foods.
Not allowed: any drastic purgatives, solid foods.

Fevers
Allowed: fasting, green vegetables, oranges.
Not allowed: Solid or starchy substances, bodily
exercise.

Genito-Urinary Diseases
Allowed: wheat, bread, rice, butter, milk, green veg-
etables and other light foods.
Not allowed: smoking, starchy substances, peas, beans,

potatoes, any spices or highly seasoned food and dishes.

Gout and Rheumatism
Allowed: rice, wheat products, including bread, fresh vegetables, fruit, plenty of water, garlic, tea, pungent items, lemonade.
Not allowed: peas, beans, any starchy and sugary substances, fish, milk, salt, cold water.

Nervous Problems
Allowed: butter, wheat products and bread, rice, baked potatoes, cabbage, peas, fresh fruit, plenty of water, tea, coffee, milk, cream, green vegetables.
Not allowed: exercise, fasting, pungent items, sweet wines.

Obesity
Allowed: exercise, purgatives, peas, beans, pungent and astringent items, honey, tomatoes, onions, grapes, acid fruits, hot water, honey (a lot), tea, coffee without milk or sugar.
Not allowed: wheat products, milk, fish, fats, cream, potatoes, sugar, and sweets and confections, butter, rice.

Piles
Allowed: laxatives, rice, butter, onions, green vegetables.
Not allowed: fish, starchy and heavy foods, oil, sugar, only limited amount of water.

Ulcers
Allowed: wheat products, bread, vegetables, vegetable oils.

Not allowed: heavy exertion, heavy foods, potatoes.

Details of Ayurveda medical practice, together with the drugs used, are not required to be covered here in detail. A general background, however, to Ayurveda drugs and their combinations, which would be used in the treatment of all known diseases, especially in the Indian subcontinent, could be useful.

Particular drug combinations of Ayurveda are not haphazardly applied in any way but rather are the results of long clinical observation and experiment in various parts of the Indian subcontinent over a lengthy period.

The Ayurveda medicines are similar in their number to drug combinations given at hospital pharmacies and prescribed at doctors' surgeries throughout the Western world in allopathic medicine. However, unlike the latter, it would be quite difficult, if not impossible, to improve on these specific Ayurveda combinations.

Emphasis on specificality may be questioned or possibly objected to by non-Ayurveda doctors. This situation may be because modern European medicine has only a limited number of specifics. New drugs are coming on to the market all the time, many of which are variations of previous drugs.

As already seen, modern European medicine and Ayurveda have different visions of medicine. The position appears to be that while the West are continually trying to find out, obtain and manufacture drugs and medicines based on the pathology of infection, usually a variable factor, Ayurveda aims always to direct its attention to the pathology of constitution, a fixed factor. While the causative factor of a disease may vary, when looked upon from different angles, the specific situation, or rather the symptom-complex factors that are presented in a disease at each stage, is more or less fixed.

In the wide-ranging material available in Ayurveda, it can be seen that any disease can now be treated. Preparations include: *kadhas, succus, asavas, aristas, churnas* and *rasayans*. The Ayurveda practitioner chooses from these and many others, in mixtures or separately, in whatever he or she would need for the patient.

Kadhas are those in which roots, barks and leaves of fresh plants are cut up and boiled in water of a volume between eight or sixteen times, and then boiled again so that the end extract is equal to $1/8$ or $1/16$ of the original volume. These *kadhas* are quite mild but effective, and completely safe, even in large doses. In Ayurveda there is a way of preserving the mixtures for a long time, without the use of alcohol or other preservatives.

Succus are the juices obtained from fresh plants and then are preserved by a special process which keeps the active ingredients for a long time.

Asavas is obtained from roots, leaves or barks of plants cut into pieces and mixed with water, honey and raw sugar. This mixture is then allowed to ferment. These medicated spirituous preparations are mild yet active. The action of almost all *asavas* is laxative, stimulative and tonic; they do not upset the liver system, although their use may be continued for quite a long time.

Next come the *aristas* group, made up of the essential parts of ready-prepared fresh drugs. They are similar to *asavas* but stronger as they have been specially prepared from the extract of drugs.

Churnas are powders and have been prepared from dry substances such as roots, leaves and barks of fresh plants. These have been reduced to a fine powder and then mixed together to form the *churnas*. The resulting powders are mostly taken with *ghee* (clarified butter), honey or milk. If not with these, then they are taken with water, where no other direction has been given. *Churnas* that have been prepared without the assistance of machinery are most effective.

Gutica and *vati* are pills to be swallowed as they are, or possibly chewed. Prepared from the powders of the various plants, barks, extracts and other medicinal agents, they are initially mixed with water, honey, sugar or guggul to form a vehicle for the preparation of the pills. These preparations, being compressed, are suitable when travelling. The pills would normally be administered with water or honey, along with any other preparation for the same condition or disease.

The next preparation is *bhasmas*, which is the ashes of reduced metal. Ordinary metals, including gold, silver and copper, are firstly purified in vegetable oils and the juices of various plants. This mixture is roasted and oxidised, then reduced to such a condition that the resultant particles of the final mixture will be able to float on the water. This 'floating on water', called *varitara*, is an important test from the medication point of view. Such *bhasmas* are easily assimilated into the general body system, and in their subsequent action on the endocrine glands. The doses are generally given with honey, *ghee*, or sugar and butter.

Important preparations in Ayurveda are those of the *rasayanas* class; instructions are strictly laid down as to their preparation in the literature of Ayurveda, by the *rishis* (seers). Each preparation in *rasayanas* will contain mercury and sulphur, in addition to the properties of fresh juices of indigenous plants. A good and skilful Ayurveda practitioner can obtain good results when using different bases in these *rasayanas*.

A variation of *rasayanas* is known as *kupistha rasayanas*, which differs in one main respect. This is the requirement for it to be heated in hard glass in a very hot furnace for a period of between 24 and 72 hours. This preparation is then stronger and more effective than the ordinary preparation.

Another preparation is *pakas*. This is a jelly-like preparation of drugs in either a paste or solid mass, and will be given with sugar or honey, giving it an agreeable taste and enabling the drug to be preserved, where necessary.

Avalehas is a linctus or extract. It is also a jelly-like preparation, and is made into a paste, with the addition of honey, sugar, powders and decoctions. The result can be swallowed in small doses, so as to act in a easy and slow way on the throat and air passages.

Muranbas are preparations which can be described as confections and consists of drugs or fruits that are prepared by soaking them in syrup or honey.

Tailas are medicated oils and consist of drugs having been boiled in water, milk or in other suitable substances, and mixed with oil. This mixture is then heated, until the water or liquid content has boiled off. The resultant oils are useful for local external application.

Ghritas is medicated *ghee*. The usual method of preparation is to boil the decoctions of specific vegetable drugs or powder in ghee.

Malamas are ointments in a semi-solid or soft state, containing the active drugs that have been mixed with *ghee*, vaseline, bees' wax, coconut oils, etc, and are used for local application. This is the basis for all ointments.

Lepas, or plasters, are prepared by mixing various resinous substances together, and applying to the affected parts with hot water, lemon juice, *ghee* or egg mixed.

Drugs are sometimes prepared in syrup form, containing a quantity of refined sugar. This is for preservation purposes, and will also make the administration of the medicine more agreeable to take.

It is a fact that Indian medicines are cheap, widely available and within reach of most people in the Indian subcontinent, including those who are poor, or on a very low income. Ayurveda could reach an even wider mass of the whole population if in the past it had obtained more support from the central and state Governments.

The Prime Minister of India, Mr A B Vajpayee, speaking at the 55th Plenary Session of the All-India Ayurveda Congress held in New Delhi in July 1998, said that the Indian systems of medicine, including Ayurveda, were the only alternatives to meet the country's health care needs. Without the help of the Indian systems it was an impossible task. Mr Vajpayee also stressed that Indian systems of medicine were capable of curing disease by attacking the root cause.

15

Good and Healthy Foods

Many factors are involved in the cooking and presentation of good food; also quantity and quality of food are important. In Ayurveda, food combination, the time of day, the season, and other factors are all taken into account. A selection of healthy foods is given below.

Rice
In the UK, rice has become an important food, as it is in combination with other foods in the cuisines of India and China. Having a nature sweet and cooling, it is also sweet in its post-digestive effect and is light. It will subdue *dosha pitta*.

Wheat
This basic food is sweet and cool. A heavier food, and strengthening.

Lentils and Peas
By their nature they are astringent and sweet. Cool and light – pungent after digestion. Subdues *pitta* and *kapha*. Will dry the body, therefore increasing *vata*.

Apples
Raw apples tend to increase *vata*; in the digestive system they help in binding foods together.

Dates
These are sweet, heavy and cool, and good for building of the body.

Figs
These are sweet, strengthening, heavy, laxative and cool. When used with nuts or chopped nuts, they are good for the building of muscle. Controls *vata* and *pitta*.

Apricots
A favourite food in the north-west Himalayas, supplying a great deal of nourishment in the form of protein, carbohydrate, sodium, calcium, magnesium, phosphorous, sulphur, copper, iron and chlorine.

Bananas
The sweet and ripe banana is a tasty fruit, flesh building and thirst quenching. It can increase the weight of people who are considered to be underweight. It will also increase vitality and virility.

Grapes
These are sweet, cooling and strengthening. Grapes help the intestines and those having weak intestines should eat a lot of them. They contain vitamins, phosphorous, calcium, minerals, but little fat or protein. An excellent all-round food.

Lemons
Heavy, strong and acidic. A good appetiser and digestive. Also a powerful antiseptic. Will subdue *kapha*.

Mangoes
An important fruit, especially in India. The ripe mango is laxative, diuretic and cools the blood, subduing *vata*. It is strengthening.

Oranges
Promotes good digestion. Harder to digest, but subdues *vata*.

Peaches
These are heavy, sweet, tasty, strengthening and easy to digest.

Tamarinds
Sour before and after digestion and hot. Good for digestion and also to increase the appetite. Has a laxative effect.

Nuts
Most nuts are sweet, heavy, hot, oily and strengthening. They are good for body building, subduing *vata* and increasing *pitta* and *kapha*.

Milk (Cow's)
Milk was regarded by Charaka as among the best substances you can have. The regard Ayurveda has for milk is that it is the very essence of plant nutrients, and concentrated into the white essence of mother cow we know so well. It is slow on the digestion, cooling, nutritious, strengthening and vitalising. It is also of a soothing and softening nature. Where cow's milk is very fresh it is among the world's best vitalisers and rejuvenators.

Legumes
These play an important part in Ayurveda and in diet. In

the Ayurveda diet, which is mainly vegetarian, where does all the protein come from to fill the need? The answer is mainly in legumes, beans and peas.

The amount of protein in the mung bean, probably the most commonly used bean in India, is up to twenty-five per cent of its total weight, which is a good percentage. A similar proportion is obtained from a large number of legumes, of which there are up to twenty to thirty different types available in the UK. A number of them are available only through the specialist Indian grocery stores, but these can be found in almost every sizeable town in the country.

Usually there are detailed instructions printed on the individual packets of the beans and peas. For example, for mung beans (sometimes spelt moong) there is the usual analysis of the energy, protein, carbohydrate and fat content, and often a recipe suggestion for a delicious vegetarian dish. It is usual to add other items, such as turmeric powder, mixed spices powder, ginger, chilli powder and coriander.

Mung beans are among the best of all the legumes. They are light, dry and act as a purifier. Of an oily nature, astringent, sweet, and cool, they will subdue *pitta* and *kapha*.

Other beans available are: chickpea, blackeyed bean, red split lentil (dal), kidney bean, soya bean, split yellow ochre lentil (dal), black garam, Indian bake bean.

Meat
Charaka said that for those who were wasted and desirous of increased strength, meat juice was to be regarded as nectar itself. Overall, he was emphatic that meat should not be used on a regular basis. Even where use of meat was required in the case of weakness, it was said to best be regarded as essentially a condiment, and consumed as a broth or soup, rather than as a steak or chop.

Vegetables

It is generally regarded that most, if not all, vegetables are good for you, but there is a qualification to this statement in Ayurveda. Although vegetables have many different qualities and characteristics, they also have different effects on the digestive system, during and after eating, and in their post-digestive effect.

Taking the position in Ayurveda as a whole, there are vegetables that grow underground, those growing and maturing near the ground, and those maturing above the ground. Vegetables growing underground include root vegetables of various kinds, including beetroot, carrots, parsnips, radishes, swedes and turnips. These are heavy in their nature, and earthy and will, on average, subdue *vata dosha* but increase *kapha* and *pitta*. Leafy vegetables, including spinach, lettuce, cabbage and squashes, will be good for *kapha* and *pitta*, meaning that these will help in subduing these *doshas*, but not so good for *vata*, as these will cause an increase in that *dosha*. This illustrates the reason why people with a *vata* constitution do not usually like leafy foods too much, or if they do, they can run into trouble with the *doshas* upsetting them. Hot pungent vegetables, including radishes are best for *vata* and *kapha*, and cucumber better for *pitta*, being a cool vegetable. Asparagus is a very good vegetable in terms of Ayurveda. Three vegetables that also come in for special mention are garlic, ginger and onion.

Garlic

This vegetable is renowned throughout the world for its qualities. Its pedigree not only relates to the modern world, it is also mentioned in the ancient writings of the Egyptians, Romans, Greeks and Chinese and other civilisations. In the old Sanskrit writings, garlic was made fun of, and described, among other things, as 'disgusting', and 'lacking one taste', the latter because garlic contains five of the six tastes, and is lacking only sour taste. The different tastes are contained in the several parts of the whole plant, including the root. Garlic subdues *vata* and *kapha*, and increases *pitta*. It is considered heavy, and an aphrodisiac. Being also antiseptic, it gives strength and can improve vision, complexion, digestion, and is good for tissue formation. It is reputed to have been used by the British Army in France during the First World War as an antiseptic in dressing wounds and checking the spread of infection. Garlic has been used to cure or improve many different diseases. The juice of garlic has the quality and ability to kill harmful bacteria without destroying useful ones. It also helps in appetite and circulation. When taken orally it is able to penetrate all parts of the body quickly.

Ginger
One of the three foods that is considered to be excellent all round. It is pungent, sweet, and sweet after digestion, and hot. It helps digestion and has a balancing effect on all three *doshas*, which in itself is a good thing. If taken to excess there is a possibility of it increasing *pitta*, and having an unbalancing effect of that *dosha*. Ginger can be powdered, or whole, the latter being used mainly for cooking purposes. In ancient times, ginger was known as the satisfaction killer, for its strength in giving increased appetite. From a medical point of view, it can be applied to the body and also used in bathing, to help circulation, give general warmth and help in relaxing muscles and relief to muscle and skeletal aches and pains.

Onion
This vegetable is strengthening, heavy and appetising. It is sweet, pungent, hot in potency, and the post-digestive effect

is sweet. Generally, it will depend on the variety of onion being used, but the redder type is more *pitta* producing than the white one. It has numerous good medical qualities observed in Ayurveda, stimulating the heart, producing bile and relieving gas and colic. In India, both its juice and paste forms are made into numerous home remedies.

Butter
Although butter contains a large proportion of fat, there is no doubt that our grandparents delighted in using it. However, because of its high-fat content and much-publicised connection with cholesterol-related diseases, there has been a move against using it in a significant way. In much wider use in India is *ghee*, that is, clarified butter.

Ghee
This is butter that has been heated and filtered. In this heating, the fat content sinks to the bottom and is not used. Ayurveda maintains that *ghee* is better than butter as its qualities change during the conversion process. It is described in Ayurveda as a lubricant for the whole system and especially the blood vessels, and is reputed to delay the ageing process. Charaka remarked that *ghee* is the best of all unctuous substances. It subdues both *vata* and *pitta*. Cow's *ghee* is sweet both before and after digestion, cool, promotes memory, intelligence, digestive fire, semen, nutrients for the body and fat. In Ayurvedic practice it is used as a basis to contain other medicines, and also in its own right.

Yoghurt
Yoghurt is a good appetiser and helps digestion. It is nourishing, gives strength and is also aphrodisiac. Being both

sweet, sour and hot in nature, and also sour after digestion, it will subdue *vata* and increase *pitta* and *kapha*.

Fats and Oils
Other than the wonderful food of *ghee*, oils are used both externally in Ayurveda and for cooking. Vegetable oils are more *rajas* and *tamas* in their effect upon the user, but *ghee* usually creates *sattva*. Mustard oil is used very much in India for cooking purposes.

Sweets
Sugar is good in controlled amounts, helps in giving energy and also in the free flow of urine. Unrefined types are good, especially both light and dark kinds of muscovado sugar. The latter are produced by pressing out the natural juice from the sugar cane, then cleaning and crystallising. This sugar contains also the natural molasses of the sugar cane. The goodness in honey is well known; it is both drying and astringent, aphrodisiac and strengthening.

Spices
These are medicinal herbs, and have the important function of not only adding taste to the food, but also altering the qualities in the food, making them more digestible. A number of well-known spices are described here.

Black Pepper
Once described as one of the world's most perfect foods. It subdues both *kapha* and *vata*, with only a slight increase in the *dosha pitta*. Black pepper is pungent, also hot and pungent after digestion.

Caraway

This is pungent and bitter, hot and also pungent after digestion. It subdues both *vata* and *kapha,* and there is a tendency for it to increase *pitta.*

Cardamom

Sweet, pungent and hot, but it does not increase *pitta dosha.* It helps the fire element (*agni*) in the digestion and will subdue all three of the *doshas,* and is considered to help in the rejuvenation of the entire system.

Chillies

These are pungent and also hot and pungent in their post-digestive effect. They reduce *vata* and *kapha* and increase *pitta.* Taking chillies during hot weather will help in the cooling of the body by inducing sweat production, but their overuse is not a good thing, as the system can become overheated.

Cinnamon

This is pungent, sweet and bitter, and is hot in its influence. The post-digestive effect is sweet; it controls *vata* and *kapha* and does not increase *pitta* unless it is taken in excess.

Coriander

The leaves and fruit are not very pungent, and are cooling. It will improve appetite, subduing *vata, pitta* and *kapha.*

Cumin

It is pungent, rather hot, and pungent after digestion. It controls *vata* and *kapha,* and will not produce *pitta* unless used in excess.

Fennel

The young shoots of fennel are used as a vegetable in India. The seeds are sweet, pungent and bitter, and also sweet in their post-digestive effect. They will subdue all the *doshas*.

Fenugreek

The seeds are pungent, bitter and sweet, hot and pungent after digestion. They subdue *vata* and *kapha* and, in excess, will increase *pitta*. They are excellent for the stimulation of the appetite, and also good for the respiratory and nervous systems.

Mustard

Helps in digestion and is a good blood purifier, assisting in the production of red blood cells. Subdues *pitta* and *kapha*.

Saffron

It is pungent, bitter and sweet, hot and sweet after digestion, and controls all the *doshas*, that is *vata*, *pitta*, and *kapha*. Regarded as an aphrodisiac.

Turmeric

A good blood purifier. It is bitter, astringent and pungent, hot, and is pungent after digestion. Subdues *vata* and *kapha* but, if used in excess, can increase *pitta*.

16
Natural Health

The aim in Ayurveda is to create the condition in the human body of well-being and good health so that, however excellent the work of orthodox and Western medicine, with its wonderful discoveries, treatments and drugs, the need for drugs or surgery is lessened.

If food and diet are right, we are then maintaining the essential balancing of the *doshas vata*, *pitta* and *kapha*. People who develop a discomfort or imbalance, as described in Ayurveda, will find that often this has not arrived on the scene all of a sudden, but has been built up gradually, creating conditions that are almost taken for granted, and forcing us to believe that such things are automatic and inevitable. There is no reason why this should be so.

In the UK, we are given a particular medicine or drug and often it works. This approach can usually be applied in general terms only, notwithstanding that each individual, and the causes for the condition within that individual, will vary and be different for each person. The medical profession's attitude can have the effect of our bodies losing their sensitivity, and encourage us to ignore the first signs of discomfort and disease. Various drugs are given, sometimes at late stages, and when the repair is going to take more time to return us to health. In some early stages of preventative medicine, a balancing diet can help prevent a person of going into ill health, or later suffering a partial or complete breakdown in health.

Vinoba Bhave once referred to people who have fixed positions on all sorts of subjects, in fact on almost every topic under the sun. He went on to say that as well as people naturally having firm faith, say in religion, there were people who had blind unbelief, as well, in a specific idea, religion, or philosophy.

Today there appears to be a large amount of uniformity in the way we act and react to situations in work and towards institutions. Many people are joiners of one sort or another, whether it is of a club, political party, a cultural or educational course, and we are comfortable about this. We are in fact great 'joiners'; this can give us a sense of belonging to whatever company, group or organisation it might be. This joining can create the good feeling of being part of a group and we achieve a sense of satisfaction in the job, profession, or organisation to which we belong. Often there is no harm in this, but care needs to be taken in terms of our well-being and health, both mental and physical. We can also be caught up in the grip of powerful consumerism, and in this respect can be affected and controlled by outside forces, perhaps more so than we would care to admit.

In this process, we often take on attitudes, mannerisms and the style of clothing adopted by a particular group, or to whom we want to relate and belong to. We thereby obtain satisfaction and a security in group activity.

Ayurveda states that well-being and healing in the body is a natural process contained in itself, given the opportunity. The primordial energy, or *prana*, is contained naturally within the body from birth but, unfortunately, this energy can be distorted, destroyed, hindered, sidetracked and systematically reduced to a feeble representation of its full force. Reduction can be caused by a variety of factors, including drugs, pills, antibiotics, painkillers, acid reducers, sleeping tablets, uppers, downers, and other devices almost too numerous to mention.

Such factors help in reducing distress and in the attempt to regain our health. Our immediate concern is in obtaining relief and to receive comfort. At the time and under such circumstance we are not concerned in getting to grips with the root cause of the disease. We fail to come face-to-face with the question as to how we arrived at ill health in the first place.

Ayurveda deals directly with the cause, realising that there is a very good chance of finding the answer. It is true to say that we suffer more problems through falling into bad or incorrect ways of living than from the troubles and effects of actual diseases. Today there are many stress-related illnesses, and the percentage of beds taken in hospitals by stress-related illnesses and mental problems is high. No doubt a lot of stress can be caused by breakdowns in personal relationships and numerous outside factors over which we have no control. These mentally related problems may be more widespread than at first realised, as many of the so-called physical problems and illnesses are believed to have a mental basis to them.

Ayurveda says that all aspects of the human personality, the physical, mental and spiritual aspects, all go to make up the whole person, and no one part can be ignored. According to Ayurveda, and in much of Eastern philosophy, there is recognition of the direct relationship between the self of a person, all other people, and the universe.

Therefore human consciousness is a fragment and an inescapable part of a universal or natural consciousness.

This relationship can be realised, either partially or wholly; there are many paths leading to a realisation, which sometimes can be achieved quickly but, in many cases, is a slower and more gradual process.

Ayurveda exists to help in achieving a balance of the various forces, and a good diet aims to obtain a balance of the three *doshas*. Ayurveda is assisting nature in its healing power and obtaining the right balance in the body through diet. Ayurveda provides the knowledge to help us to use the means of our everyday diet to do so.

Meditation and concentration is also contained in Ayurveda, and the importance of both are stressed. The mind can be gathered into a state of quietness, at least for a short period each day, notwithstanding many distractions. Many are already practising Hatha Yoga, the physical postures, and there are thousands of classes on yoga being regularly attended throughout the country. Other branches of yoga include Raja Yoga, dealing with the mind, Bhakti Yoga covering the practice of devotion to and love of God or the Absolute. Gnana Yoga attempts to deal with the questions concerning life and the riddle of the universe. Karma Yoga, for example, shows the way through service and work. All these different branches of yoga are paths to the goal of self-realisation.

In balancing the three essential forces of *vata*, *pitta* and *kapha*, there are three stages to consider. The first is a state of discomfort, and not being at ease with ourselves. The next stage the need to put a name to this discomfort, which then comes under a name recognised as a disease or condition. Lastly, we find the means of eliminating or suppressing this disease or condition.

We know when health exists; there is no need to tell us. We are in a state where there is no discomfort, in relation to our physical and mental conditions. Always present are psychological, spiritual, material and economic aspects in our circumstances. These factors do play a part, although sometimes we may not realise it.

The contribution of food and nutrition towards offering a solution to ailments needs a higher priority in the United Kingdom. The situation now appears to be getting better, however, as regular information is given through the media from the main medical organisations and the Ministry of Health and Social Security.

The main work of the medical profession is rightly to prescribe medicines and courses of treatments, including surgery where appropriate. In no way is this book a criticism of the medical profession; there is no doubt of the enormous amount of life-saving work and general care provided by doctors in general practice and by scores of hospitals up and down the country, not forgetting all the other workers in the health service. This good work has continued throughout the whole of the last century, and advances in medical practices are continually being made.

The problem is that in cases of ill health and disease, the initial symptoms may or may not disappear or subside, and both the condition and discomfort may persist. The original condition may also develop into another symptom or condition. This is one of the outstanding problems of today. Ayurveda has been saying for a long time that we must become increasingly aware of the ways in which a condition or discomfort arises. We want and feel the need to be in a state of well-being. We deserve and expect a better deal for ourselves.

17

The Way Ahead

In Ayurveda the utmost importance is placed on the diagnosis, the disturbance or vitiation of the *doshas* that has been brought about. This diagnosis will always be foremost in the Ayurvedic doctor's mind and form the basis of that doctor's reaction.

The strength in Ayurveda lies not only in the positive approach of the diagnosis but also in the consideration that is given to the patient in totality, his or her temperament, habits, background and environment, the influence of family background, heredity and overall constitution.

Health is considered to be the foundation of virtue, wealth, enjoyment and salvation. Ayurveda is concerned with the work of obtaining and maintaining to that health, wellness and well-being of each person. The mere removal of the causative factors of the disease may not always result in its total removal, and the effects of the disease may remain in operation. Therefore much emphasis is given to the prevention of the recurrence of the condition and the returning to the proper functioning of the body systems.

Ayurveda has always stressed the importance of diet in health. As we have seen, this will also have its effect on the Ayurvedic drugs given, where the complete therapy of

Ayurveda is carried out. Take, as an example, the condition *Amavata* which, in modern terms, is rheumatoid arthritis. There are several dietary measures suggested to reduce *ama* formation and to improve digestion. These will include total fasting, and special diet combinations, including meat and milk products, citrus fruits and milk. The inclusion of bitter foods, the importance of garlic and other spices will also be put forward as being beneficial.

What has been increasingly reported over the past decade is the importance of our immune system and its vital relationship in health and disease. The immune system is a state, and in Ayurveda it is its objective to work at balancing the three *doshas*. When balancing occurs, it will give a more desirable and healthier way of living, and lead to the wellness of each individual.

In Ayurveda, there are two main classes of disorders or diseases. The first of these is in respect of those within the human body, arising from improper diet and other practices. The second main group are those conditions caused by external injury. The latter are the so-called adventitious diseases, including cuts, falls and shocks of various kinds. We also have a whole range of infectious diseases and these also are regarded as adventitious. On the other hand, Ayurveda notes that even here the *dosha* equilibrium in the individual has in some way been disturbed, thus allowing or causing the condition or disease. Where there is loss of equilibrium of the three *doshas*, the outside factor or agent will affect the person.

This is demonstrated often during epidemics and in infectious diseases, when some people will be affected and others, fortunately the majority in many cases, are not affected at all or perhaps only to a limited extent. Ayurveda believes that, although there will be other factors at work, i.e. inoculation, immunity is greatly helped when the *doshas* in the individual are in equilibrium. The loss of this protective immunity can be the root cause or reason for the disease, according to Ayurveda, and not the bug or other outside agent. When the *dosha* balance is restored, the potency of the bug is annihilated and the illness or disease reduces and disappears. Epidemics are the result of the loss of this equilibrium in the universal counterparts of the human *doshas*, the three metaphysical forces of the universe, *sattva, rajas* and *tamas*. Therefore it follows logically that germs are the result of the derangement in *doshas*.

From a medical point of view the treatment of mental disease forms an integral part in Ayurveda, the science of life. These diseases are divided into two main categories, those that are partly mental and partly physical and, secondly, purely mental diseases. The partly mental include types of insanity, epilepsy, etc. which will influence the mind and body at the same time. The purely mental problems and diseases, involving lack of *dosha* balance, are excessive anger, grief, fear, joy, despondency, depression, envy, misery, pride, greed, lust, desire, malice, etc. This list is extremely interesting and important, describing fairly the problems in society today and their causes. It is even more interesting, when you realise that this list was written in fifth to fourth centuries BC by the Ayurveda master, Sushruta.

And Charaka writes: 'The mental disorders should be cured by the help of imparting knowledge and developing the understanding of the patient, by soothing, or by waking up forgotten and sub-conscious ideas and by prescribing the practice of meditation, etc.' This is in line with modern medical psychoanalysis, which has conveniently come along over two thousand years later.

The Ayurveda masters had discovered germs of diseases

but even then they had the good sense not to believe them to be the actual universal cause of disease. According to them, germs are simply a condition and, given the foundation for the bacilli to grow and form the necessary culture, the disease will occur, but not otherwise.

Where the balance of the tissue (*dhatus*) is disturbed then the germs will get the upper hand. The *tridosha* theory of Ayurveda does not oppose any kind of germ theory, but rises above it, understanding and comprehending it.

Modern medicine, however, does not appear to have recognised the trend in the food industry of creating a tolerance of ordinary day-to-day food items, and which are not providing a good state of health. For example, the role of common salt causing hypertensive disease is fairly well founded. A tolerance to salt, thus created, could well lead to the urge to eat more salt. Such tolerance situations need to be further investigated by the medical profession.

There is no doubt of an increasing awareness of the importance of complementary or alternative medical systems in the UK and in other countries in Europe, especially in Poland and Germany. This being the case, Ayurveda can rightly take its place high up on the list of alternative systems, bearing in mind its long and significant history. After all, many historians throughout the world consider India to be the cradle of the human race. If this is so, it would indeed place Ayurveda at the forefront of medical knowledge.

The unique aspect of the Ayurveda system and philosophy of medicine is its total emphasis on the dietary aspects of living a healthy life. In other words, we may be free of disease, but are we feeling well, or put another way, do we feel in the state of 'wellness' that we want for ourselves.

Many problems have arisen when researching into the realms of Ayurveda therapies. In the past decade there have been increasing studies on the subject in various parts of the world, and especially so in India. There, several institutions exist where serious research is continually conducted on a regular and ongoing basis, one of the leading ones being the Institute of Medical Sciences of Benares Hindu University, Varanasi.

There is no doubt much more research and verification of the concepts of Ayurveda are needed. Fortunately, with the advancing interest being shown in Ayurveda, there is a unique opportunity for further research to be carried out, using state-of-the-art technical and creative facilities available at so many universities and other research centres throughout the world. In January 1999, the Indian National Award of Padma Shri for distinguished service in any field, including government employees, was given to three people working in Ayurveda: Mr Devendra Triguna (Medicine-Ayurvedic), New Delhi; Dr Panniyanipalli Krishna Warrier (Medicine-Ayurvedic), Kottskkal; and Mr Vaidya Balendu Prakash (Medicine-Ayurvedic), Dehra Dun.

With the advances in technology, much of the phenomena that has been so wonderfully described in the ancient texts can now be verified. For example, a fundamental concept in Ayurveda is that when there has been a vitiation of *dosha* on the micro-environment of cells, making themliable to damage, this can well lead to disease.

Health is in no way synonymous with the absence of disease, or even with the absence of any disturbing symptoms. What health in Ayurveda really means is the essential matter of the completely good integration of all body systems, as maintained by the bio-regulatory functions within that body. What Ayurveda reveals is that there is no earthly reason why these internal body systems, in other words the *doshas*, cannot be regulated or mobilised in a variety of ways, particularly in having a proper system of diet. Where an imbalance of the *doshas* is occurring, then the application of a number of different therapeutic methods and techniques comes into play. It is therefore within the realms of obtaining wellness for the individual, and maintaining this wellness continually, that Ayurveda exists. It is here that one of the greatest contributions can be offered by the system of Ayurveda, and also through the many other forms of complementary therapeutic systems throughout the world. Ayurveda is not the only system, there are many others.

When looking into Ayurveda we realise that Ayurveda is a deep subject indeed; in reality, a bridge between science, religion, reason and faith. In other words, it is a unique mix of body, mind and spirit. Ayurveda has the goal of leading us forward in its aim of giving us a happier and healthier life.

The name Ayurveda says it all – the science of life and its knowledge of healthy living. It is not merely confined to defeating illness and disease. Its purpose and scope is much wider.

A great deal of wonderful work is being continually carried out in the National Health Service in the UK, but at a cost of around fifty billion pounds a year and rising. There is no doubt of the vast vested interests that surround the health-care industry. However, there is still great hope for the future as everyone wants to feel well in the first place, if not all or at least most of the time. Fortunately, people are now more aware of the role food and diet has to play.

We can substantially increase good health and well-being by making adjustments to our food and diet when needed and by keeping the all important *doshas* of *vata*, *pitta* and *kapha* in order. This action is simply taken by making changes in the choice of interesting and enjoyable building blocks of the body – that is, food.

We know the *doshas*, we know the different tastes in food, we know the *dosha* qualities in each type of food, and also the other qualities that are in the food. Having the knowledge of our own constitution, we have the means and the key to our own well-being, and to enjoy ourselves along the way.

We cannot lose.

Glossary

Agni	Fire of life, digestion
Agnimandya	Diminished digestion
Akash	Space
Albuminoids	Proteins for body energy
Ama	Improperly digested food particles
Amla Rasa	Sour taste
Apa	Water
Asthi	Bone
Asthidhatu	Bone, or skeleton support
Bhakti	Yoga practice of love and devotion to God, Absolute
Bhavana	Offering
Brahma	God, Absolute, Almighty
Cartesian	Method of scientific materialism
Dhatus	Tissues, support
Dosha	Elements that control the various functions in the body, i.e. *vata*, *pitta* and *kapha*

Ghee	Clarified butter
Gita	*The Song Celestial*, or *Bhagavad Gita*, an ancient scripture
Gnana Yoga	Concerning life and riddle of the universe
Gunas	Sole constituents of the manifested universe, i.e. *sattva, rajas* and *tamas*
Guru vipaka	Heavy foods
Hatha Yoga	Physical postures and exercises
Hing	Asafoetida
Jatharagni	Most important *agni*, influencing the character of all other *agnis*, thereby altering the functions of the cells
Kapha	The *dosha* element of earth and water, predominant in childhood
Karma Yoga	Realisation through service and work
Kashaya	Astringent taste
Katu	Hot, spicy taste
Kayachikitsa	Treatment for the body, when digestion and proper assimilation of food have gone wrong
Laghu vipaka	Light foods
Lavana	Salt taste
Madhur rasa	Sweet taste
Mahbharata	Famous epic written by the sage Vyas, of which the *Gita* is a part
Maiakriya	Metabolic end-products

Majjadhatu	Includes the bone marrow and the nervous tissue
Mala	Metabolic end-products
Mamsadhatu	Flesh and muscles
Medadhatu	Fat tissue
Methi	Green leafy vegetables, or seeds, fenugreek
Moong	Type of pulse or legume, or mung
Moong dal	Lentil
Ojas	Nutrients, ultimate product of metabolism
Panchamahabhoota	The five-element theory
Pitta	Dosha element made up of fire and water
Prajnaparadha	Violation of good sense, crimes against wisdom
Prakriti	Constitution, in humans; unmanifested ground of the universe
Prana	Energy
Prithvi	Earth
Purusha	Absolute
Raga	Desire, heat, passion
Rajas	Quality of passion, heat, characterised by a tendency to do work or overcome resistance
Rajastic	Activity
Raja Yoga	Branch of yoga dealing with the mind and mental development
Raktadhatu	The blood
Ramayana	Ancient Hindu scripture

Rasa	Taste. Also refers to liquid, potion, nectar, essence, sap, every juice that makes life possible and worth living
Rasadhatu	Primordial tissue, nourishes and influences other tissues it bathes
Reals	Qualities, or *gunas*, of *sattva, rajas* and *tamas*
Rishis	Seers
Samskara	Tendency developed by repeated action
Samskaras	Repeated actions
Sara	Well-digested food
Sattva	Quality of goodness, light medium for reflection of intelligence
Sattvic	Lightness in nature
Shukradhtu	Represents the seed, the sperm or egg
Soonth	Dried ginger
Srotas	Channels
Tamas	Quality of darkness, inertia, mass
Tamasic	Heavy in its nature
Tattwas	The five elements of earth (solid state), water (liquid state), fire (transforming state), air (gaseous state), ether (simultaneously the source of all matter and the space in which it exists)
Tikta rasa	Bitter taste
Tridosha	Theory of the three *doshas*, i.e. *vata, pitta* and *kapha*
Tulsi	Basil plant

Unanni	System of medecine introduced by Muslim rulers
Upanishads	Ancient Sanskrit scriptures on Vedanta philosophy
Vaid	Ayurvedic physician
Varitara	Drug particles floating on water
Vata	Dosha element made up of air and space
Vayu	Air
Veda	An ancient book in Sanskrit scripture
Yajna	Sacrifice

Bibliography

Balwant Singh, Thakur and Chunek, Dr K C, *Glossary of Vegetable Drugs in Brihattrayi*, Chowkhamba Sansk, India, 1972

Bhagavat Sinh Jee, H H Maharaja of Gondal, *Aryan Medical Science: a Short History*, Rare Reprints, Delhi, 1986

Bhave, Vinoba, *Talks on the Gita*, Sarva Seva Sangh Prakashan, Varanasi, 1932, 1995

Chakraberty, Chandra, *An Interpretation of Ancient Hindu Medicine*, Low Priced Publications, Delhi, 1923, 1993

Chopra, Colonel Sir R N *et al*, *Indigenous Drugs of India*, second edition, Academic Publishers, Calcutta, 1982

Dahanukar, Sharadini and Thatte, Urmila, *Ayurveda Revisited*, Popular Prakashan, Bombay, 1989
— *Ayurveda Unravelled*, National Book Trust, New Delhi, 1996

Dash, Bhagwan, *Fundamentals of Ayurvedic Medicine*, Bansal & Co, Delhi, 1978

Filliozat, J, *The Classical Doctrine of Indian Medicine*, Munshiram Manoharlal, Delhi, 1964

Gandhi, Maneka, *Brahma's Hair*, Rupa & Co, New Delhi, 1989

Gunawant, Deepila, *The Complete Illustrated guide to Ayurveda: the ancient Indian healing tradition*. Element, Shaftesbury, 1997

Gupta, Shakti M, *Plant Myths and Traditions in India*, MRML, India, 1991

Heyn, Birgit, *Ayurveda Medicine: The Gentle Strength of Indian Healing*, Thorsons, Wellingborough, 1987

Johari, Harish, *Dhanwantari*, Rupa & Co, New Delhi, 1992

Kirtikar, K R and Basu, B D, *Indian Medicinal Plants*. Four volumes of text, plus four volumes containing 1,053 pages and 1,033 plates with line drawings, eight volumes in all, Bishen Singh, 1935, 1989, India

Krishnamurthy, K H, *Wealth of Sushruta*, International Institute of Ayurveda, Coimbatore, 1991

— editor, Health Series, *Traditional Family Medicine: Harad and Baheda*; *Gourds and Pumpkins*; *Amalaka and Bhumi Amalaka*; *Onion and Garlic*; *Neem and its Relatives*; *Banyan and Peepul*; *Khas, Kesar, Nagakesar and Khaskhas*; *Coconut, Supari, Kikar and Catha*; *Bael, Wood Apple, Lemons and Castor*; *Ginger and Turmeric*; *Salts, Sugar, Jaggery and Honey*; *Spices*; *Isabgol, Gokhru and Brahmi*; *Seasoning Herbs*; *Fragrant Herbs*; *Milk and Milk Products*; *Leafy Vegetables*; *Vegetables*; *Fruits*; *Karatashringi, Indubar, Nausadar and Fitkari*, Books for All, Delhi, 1997 (20 books)

Kutumbiah, Dr P, *Ancient Indian Medicine*, Orient Longmans, Madras, 1962

Lad, Vasant, *Ayurveda, the Science of Self-Healing*, second edition, Lotus Press, Santa Fe, US, 1985

Lad, Vasant and Frawley, David, *The Yoga of Herbs: an Ayurveda Guide to Herbal Medicine*, Lotus Press, Santa Fe, 1986

Lele, Dr R D, *Ayurveda and Modern Science*, BVB, India, 1986

Mehta, P M, editor, *Charaka Samhita*, Gulab Kunverba Society, Gujarat, India, 1949

Mooss, Vayaskara N S, *Ayurveda Flora Medica*, Vaidyasarathy Press, Kottayam, Kerala, India, 1978

Mukhopadhyaya, Girindranath, *History of Indian Medicine*, Oriental Books Reprint Corporation, New Delhi, 1974

Patel, Ramesh, *The Mandeer Ayurveda Cook Book*, Curzon Press Ltd, 1997

Pflug, Bernd, *Education in Ayurveda: a Reconstructional Analysis*, Gian, India, 1992

Ranade, Professor Dr Subhash, *National Healing Through Ayurveda*, MLBD, India, 1994

Ray, P and Gupta, H N, *Charaka Samhita: a Scientific Synopsis*, National Institute of Sciences of India, New Delhi, 1965

Sachs, Melanie, *Ayurveda Beautycare: the Ageless Techniques to Invoke Natural Beauty*, MLBD, India, 1995

Sandu, D V, *Indian Therapeutic*, Sri Satguru Publications, Delhi, 1987

Schutt, Karen, *Ayurveda, the Secret of Lifelong Youth*, Time-Life Books, Amsterdam, 1997

Seal, Dr Brajendranath, *The Positive Sciences of the Ancient Hindus*, Motilal Banarisdas, Delhi, 1958

Sharma, Pandit Shiv, *Realms of Ayurveda*, Arnold-Heinemann, India, 1979

Sharma, P V, *Fruits and Vegetables in Ancient India*, Chaukhambha Orientalia, Varanasi, 1979

— *Charaka Samhita*, four volumes, Chaukhambha Orientalia, Varanasi, 1988, 1992

— *Descriptive Catalogue of Manuscripts on Ayurveda*, BHU, India 1984

Sharma, S, *The System of Ayurveda*, Low Price Publications, Delhi, 1929

Singha, Shyam, *The Secrets of Natural Health*, Element Books, Shaftesbury, 1997

Svoboda, Robert E, *Ayurveda: Life, Health and Longevity*, Penguin Books, India, 1993

— *Prakruti: Your Ayurvedic Constitution*, Geocom, Albuquerque, US, 1988

Varier, Vaidyaratnam, *Indian Medicinal Plants: a Compendium of 500 Species*, vol. 1, 1993, Vol. 2, 1994, Orient-Longman, India (two further volumes to come)

Wise, T A, *The Hindu System of Medicine*, Mittal, Delhi, 1986

Zimmer, H R, *Hindu Medicine*, Johns Hopkin Press, Baltimore, US, 1948

Index